TWENTIETH CENTURY INTERPRETATIONS

OF

SANCTUARY

TWENTIETH CENTURY INTERPRETATIONS OF

SANCTUARY

A Collection of Critical Essays

Edited by

J. DOUGLAS CANFIELD

A SPECTRUM BOOK

Prentice-Hall, Inc., Englewood Cliffs, New Jersey 07632

Library of Congress Cataloging in Publication Data
Main entry under title:

Twentieth century interpretations of Sanctuary.

    (Twentieth century interpretations)
    "A Spectrum Book."
    Bibliography: p.
    1. Faulkner, William, 1897–1962.   Sanctuary—Ad-
dresses, essays, lectures.   I. Canfield, J. Douglas
(John Douglas) (date).   II. Series.
PS3511.A86S438   813'.52   82-7573
ISBN 0-13-791228-5   AACR2
ISBN 0-13-791210-2 (pbk.)

Editorial/production supervision by Maxine Bartow
Woodcut by Vivian Berger © 1982
Manufacturing buyer: Barbara A. Frick

10 9 8 7 6 5 4 3 2 1

ISBN 0-13-791228-5

ISBN 0-13-791210-2 {PBK.}

PRENTICE-HALL INTERNATIONAL, INC., *London*
PRENTICE-HALL OF AUSTRALIA PTY. LIMITED, *Sydney*
PRENTICE-HALL CANADA INC., *Toronto*
PRENTICE-HALL OF INDIA PRIVATE LIMITED, *New Delhi*
PRENTICE-HALL OF JAPAN, INC., *Tokyo*
PRENTICE-HALL OF SOUTHEAST ASIA PTE. LTD., *Singapore*
WHITEHALL BOOKS LIMITED, *Wellington, New Zealand*

For Bret—he prevailed

Contents

V. Structuralist Criticism

Introduction

by J. Douglas Canfield

I

It has been half a century since the publication in 1931 of William Faulkner's first popular novel, *Sanctuary*. After its immediate success, Faulkner became something of a celebrity sought after by the literary establishment in New York and the film establishment in Hollywood.[1] Despite the sensationalism of the novel which so outraged British reviewers, it received many favorable reviews in America[2] and brought Faulkner into prominence with such French intellectuals as André Malraux, Jean-Paul Sartre, Simone de Beauvoir, and Albert Camus.[3] Within a few years the novel was made into a movie as *The Story of Temple Drake*, and its enduring popularity is attested to by its many reprintings in cheap editions, a second film adaptation in 1960,[4] and Random House's decision to print in 1981 an earlier version entitled *"Sanctuary": The Original Text*, whose publication appropriately marks the novel's golden anniversary.[5]

[1] All my references are to works listed alphabetically in the Bibliography, where the reader may conveniently find full titles and publishing information. For biographical details of this period, see Blotner, I, 604 ff.

[2] For a listing of reviews, see Bassett (1972), pp. 61–65, and for a selection, see Bassett (1975), pp. 107–17.

[3] See Malraux's preface; de Beauvoir, pp. 191–93, for her and Sartre's attraction to *Sanctuary*; and Camus's letter.

[4] For the best treatment of the film adaptations, see Degenfelder.

[5] This version of the novel (cited throughout this introduction as G [galley version], simply followed by page number) Faulkner had finished typing and sent off to his publisher, Jonathan Cape and Harrison Smith, at the end of May 1929. According to many accounts Faulkner later gave, Smith wrote and said they could not publish it or they would all be in jail. Faulkner then proceeded to write *As I Lay Dying*, which was accepted immediately. To his surprise, Smith evidently had a change of mind and sent Faulkner galley proofs of *Sanctuary* in November 1930. At considerable expense Faulkner tore them down and rewrote the novel in order, he said many times later, to make it worthy of *The Sound and the Fury* and *As I Lay Dying*. The revised version was published 9 February 1931 and a year later in 1932 was reissued in a Modern Library edition. Thirty years later in 1962 the novel was reset to correct some printing errors (though some were missed, as in the clause "if that's what you're hinting it," p. 197: Faulkner's holograph manuscript, p. 96, and the carbon of his typescript, p. 251, have "hinting at"; obviously, Faulkner missed the

It was also half a century ago that Faulkner appended to the Modern Library edition of *Sanctuary* his famous Introduction, in which he maintained that he wrote the novel to make money, that accordingly he created "the most horrific tale" he could and composed it in "about three weeks."[6] Almost every critical analysis since has begun with this Introduction, the gist of which Faulkner repeated in numerous interviews,[7] and it has thus constituted the first great red herring of criticism on *Sanctuary*. Critics have felt compelled either to agree with Faulkner and disparage the novel or to argue with him and defend it. In either case, they have made a fundamental theoretical error in according his remarks a privileged status. An author is not necessarily the best judge of his motives, his meanings, or his products. Moreover, as several critics have shown, Faulkner was fibbing in at least some details (speed of composition, for instance: Faulkner took at least four months), and he appears to have written the whole Introduction with tongue in cheek. Even more important, for years criticism neglected Faulkner's claim, repeated in interview after interview, that it was the penultimate version he disliked and that he tried in his final version to make "something which would not shame *The Sound and the Fury* and *As I Lay Dying* too much." He says at the end of his Introduction that he hopes he made "a fair job," and several studies have argued that indeed he did.[8] Two recent critics have gone so far as to argue that the penultimate version is a good novel, perhaps even better than the final version itself.[9] Let us hope, however, that the time has come for us to throw this particular red herring back into the sea.

At the same time—not to refute Faulkner but to understand his craft and evaluate the finished product—a genetic study of the text of *Sanctuary* may prove useful.[10] Several pages in the manuscript are obviously yellower and considerably older than the rest. Many have been re-

error in page proofs, p. 245). The 1931 and 1962 editions of the novel and their various reprintings, especially the old Modern Library reissue of the first and the 1967 Vintage reissue of the second, are the reliable texts and are the ones cited in this collection as follows: David Williams uses the first edition; Kubie, Frazier, Vickery, Rossky, and McHaney use the Modern Library; Aubrey Williams designates no text but probably uses the Modern Library also; and Adamowski, Kinney, Toles, Weinstein, and the editor use the Vintage, which is cited throughout this Introduction as V, followed simply by page number. See the Bibliography for a listing of these texts and pre-texts under Faulkner. And see Meriwether's two articles for further textual information.

[6]The Introduction is also conveniently reprinted in Faulkner, *Essays, Speeches, and Public Letters*, pp. 176–78.

[7]See, for example, Gwynn and Blotner, pp. 90–91; Blotner, I, 670, n. to line 20; Meriwether and Millgate, pp. 54–55, 92, 122–24.

[8]See especially Massey; Millgate; and Beck, pp. 191–260.

[9]See Langford, Introduction; and Polk, Afterword to G.

[10]Professor Kingo Hanamoto of Waseda University, Toyko, is preparing a detailed study of the relationship between the manuscript and the typescript of *Sanctuary*.

numbered a dozen times or more. Many are pastiches of passages cut and pasted together. Faulkner deleted false starts in countless sentences, and he shifted the beginning of the novel time and again, once opening with the townsboys gathering to catch a glimpse of Temple at Ole Miss (ms, p. 39), at another time opening with the trial scene (ms, p. 131). Faulkner's last shift in the manuscript resulted in opening with Goodwin—actually the Negro baritone—in jail awaiting fate. This beginning Faulkner again discarded in his galley revision in favor of the juxtaposition of Horace and Popeye at the spring. Obviously, Faulkner gave the structure of the novel a great deal of care, experimenting, interchanging parts, developing new lines of narrative. His final changes in the order of the novel, then, cannot be viewed with any sense of finality. Given the chance, he might have revised again. As he often said, he was constantly trying to tell and retell a story in the hope of getting it right. Unfortunately, a genetic study of the text of *Sanctuary*, at least, leaves us no comfortable ontological illusions about the essence of a Faulkner text.

When revising his prose from manuscript to typescript, though he often deleted sentences and paragraphs or false starts of sentences, he appears hardly ever to have revised the phrasing within sentences. He seems to have had amazing confidence in a sentence once cast. There are some extraordinary passages, like the opening of Temple's narration of her night at the Old Frenchman's Place, which have not one canceled word on an uncut page and were never again altered through the final version. Still, he did revise sentences, apparently as he was typing, and he often added whole new paragraphs, evidently off the top of his head. Sometimes he spontaneously improved a joke—for example, the one about playing the "Blue Danube" at Red's funeral. In the manuscript the exchange continues:

"What's that?" the second man said.
"Rubenstein," the leader said.
"A wop?" the other said. (ms, p. 113)

The passage in the typescript is the same as that in the final version:

"No, no; don't play the blues, I tell you," the proprietor said. "There's a dead man in that bier."
"That's not blues," the leader said.
"What is it?" the second man said.
"A waltz. Strauss."
"A wop?" the second man said. (V 237)

In the same dialogue, Faulkner appears to have eliminated a Joycean pun: the proprietor fears the effects of Gene's punch and says in the manuscript, "It's going to turn this funeral into a fun-for-all" (ms, p. 113). Again, the typescript reads like the final version: "But I might have knowed somebody'd have to turn it into a carnival" (V 238). When he contemplates the logic of evil, Horace is reminded of the expression "in the eyes of a dead child." There the manuscript stops (p. 103), but the typescript continues as in the final version: "and of other dead: the cooling indignation, the shocked despair fading, leaving two empty globes in which the motionless world lurked profoundly in miniature" (V 214). Occasionally Faulkner expands a crucial dialogue, such as that between Narcissa and Eustace Graham in the District Attorney's office or that between Temple and Eustace at the trial scene. Or he completely changes his plan, as in the decision between manuscript and typescript *not* to have Horace summon Temple—a change that produced an extraordinary new section discussed in detail below.

The major revisions between penultimate and ultimate texts are of three kinds: rearrangement, addition, and deletion. Langford especially has commented on these matters, and I shall not belabor the points he has made. The major effect was to deemphasize Horace's story and to emphasize Temple's. Instead of deferring her story till midway, Faulkner moved it forward so that we are engaged in it almost immediately. He still begins with Horace, but he deletes material that treats Horace's failed marriage with Belle and his incestuous love for his sister Narcissa, his stepdaughter Little Belle, and even his mother. Also deleted are Horace's rather abstract and increasingly cynical reflections on life.

Whatever Faulkner's intentions, cutting such passages made the final version more mysterious, dramatic, and intense. The ambiguity thus created as to Horace's motives, which some critics have complained of, is in my view an asset. If Horace were guilty of an incest so blatant as to cause others to mention it explicitly and he himself to acknowledge it, his discovery of evil and his own complicity in it would have far less impact. He would already be guilty of violating a fundamental societal taboo. In the final version, Horace displays no explicit incestuous desire for Narcissa. If we suspect such a desire, it will only be because we remember the Horace of *Sartoris*. The final version subordinates incest to Horace's desire for Little Belle, a desire not literally incestuous and wholly implicit. The change is an improvement because it makes his discovery of his complicity in evil far less conscious, expressed simply in the imagery of his fantasy while vomiting (V 215–16), which the reader must *interpret* by reference to his drunken ramblings at the Old Frenchman's Place (V 13–16) and his later scene in front of the photograph of Little Belle (V 162–63). Thus in the final version, his complex sexual motivations remain submerged, and he can continue to sublimate them into a fight for justice. In this way, he becomes more sympathetic.

To the same end, Faulkner removes Horace's abstract ruminations before the trial scene and during it. For example, after Miss Reba tells Horace that Temple is gone, he reflects, "Thank God, . . . thank God. He

realised now that it was too late, that he could not have summoned her;
realised again that furious homogeneity of the middle classes when
opposed to the proletariat from which it so recently sprung and by which
it is so often threatened. Better that he should hang, he thought, than to
expose . . . . than to expose . . . . I cannot even face the picture,
he told himself" (G 260). What Horace means is clearer if we turn to a
deleted marginal interpolation in which (in the manuscript) he considers
why he does not want to use Temple's testimony unless he absolutely has
to: "It would be irrefutable but what with the ancient fashion about
chivalry toward women to which the south clung so stubbornly, despite
the efforts of the women themselves to slay it" (*sic*, ms, p. 121). What
Faulkner seems to have planned to suggest originally is that Horace
could not, finally, even to save Lee or to serve his Proletarian Madonna,
bring himself to subject Temple to cross-examination; that when pressed,
he would himself finally side with Southern respectability and its myth of
chivalry toward women; that he would remain hopelessly bourgeois,
even at the sacrifice of members of the proletariat who he knows are
better than their supposed betters. Thus his silence during Temple's
testimony could be interpreted as shock not just at *her* corruption and
that of his own sister in betraying his case but at that of Temple's family
in so crassly abandoning chivalry and allowing her not only to lie about
the murder but to tell the story of her horrible desecration and to blame
that on Lee too. But such an interpretation, among others, is still possible
without the obtrusive abstractions, especially the concept of the proletariat.[11] Here again, leaving motivation unspecific makes the novel
more dramatic, its evil less glibly catalogued, its outcome less predictable.

The same thing seems true of Temple. The second great red herring
of criticism on this novel has been the attempt to discover "What Really
Happens in *Sanctuary*,"[12] that is, why Temple perjures herself. The
problem with this kind of speculation is that it evades the important
questions. If there has been a "deal," as some think, why does Temple
agree to it? For that matter, why does Popeye, who seems to want Temple
as his moll enough to kill for her? In the final version Faulkner answers
the second question, at least symbolically. Temple is the gun Popeye

[11] Not that the novel will not sustain a Marxist analysis. See Lewis's article for an early,
aborted start in that direction; he concludes, "What you are intended to see in these scenes
[especially that of the college kids on the train] is undoubtedly the proliferation of a spoilt, a
purposeless, a common, an irresponsible bourgeois society . . ." (p. 327). Temple is "the little
sensational robot pupped by the American million-dollar-drugged capitalist system" (p.
328).
[12] Such is the title of the article by Nishiyama. For the most intelligent of these
speculations, see also Materassi, pp. 145–48, and especially Brooks, pp. 121–27. Though
Brooks is properly careful to remind us we are just speculating, he nevertheless constructs
an objectivist chronology (pp. 387–89).

sends to shoot Lee. The D.A.'s holding up of the bloodstained corncob and his report of the gynecologist's comment—"who says that this is no longer a matter for the hangman, but for a bonfire of gasoline" (V 276)—constitute the loading and cocking of the gun. The roaring bonfire is the direct hit of Popeye's revenge. The question why Temple herself agrees to the deal is still, however, left unanswered. Is she afraid of the men she keeps staring at in the back of the courtroom? Are they the same four goons who helped Popeye kill Red, now present as enforcers of the deal? Or are they her brothers, as indeed she appears to say in *Requiem for a Nun* (p. 133)? If so, why does she fear them? In any case they seem to be interchangeable with the four goons, enforcers of a deal or at least a code that defeats justice, defiles a woman's reputation, and murders an innocent man. Part of Faulkner's point is perhaps that there is no real separation between the underworld and normal society. As suggested in the narcissistic scene juxtaposing Horace and Popeye in the mirror of the spring—for two whole hours!—the two worlds merely reflect each other.[13]

Thus Temple's motivation remains cryptic. And, I would say, with reason. For the greatness of this version of *Sanctuary* lies precisely in ambiguities. Like Faulkner's other great works, it is a novel about interpretation itself, about our need to find words to name, to understand that "black and nameless threat" which Popeye represents (V 117) but which is also present in Temple, Narcissa, Horace, and society at large. In the face of the apparently senseless evil of a Popeye, or of Shakespeare's Iago, or of Melville's Claggart, we perpetually ask "Why?" seeking in Scripture or myth or philosophy or psychology some set of words that will temporarily assuage our fear of the unknown, the uncanny—the *unheimlich* (foreign, un-home-ly), as Freud called it, that frightens so much precisely because it is really *heimlich* (right here at home in us).[14]

But if Faulkner in his final version went to such pains to eliminate passages that made motivation more explicit, why did he add the passage on Popeye's background, which so many critics dislike? We can never know, but we can analyze its effects. It comes across, I think, as an

---

[13]Perhaps this mirroring of under and upper worlds would be a better starting point for a Marxist analysis than Faulkner's deleted comment about the proletariat. The underworld might be seen as simply a more efficient form of capitalist exploitation, with a sexuality no more decadent or perverse than that of middle-aged, middle-class, hedonistic, and mostly divorced America; with a morality perhaps less hypocritical; with a system of justice that also serves merely interest, power, hierarchy. The underworld simply feeds and feeds off the upper world's vices, particularly, in this novel, alcohol, a symbol of bourgeois decadence, shrouding all classes in drugged stupefaction, blinding them to the incredible price mankind pays for the maldistribution of wealth.

[14]See "The 'Uncanny'," *Imago* (1919), rpt. in Freud, pp. 122–61.

anecdotal parody of a typically modern, sociopsychological, environmental explanation. Popeye's father was a brutal, syphilitic strike breaker, who accused nameless "bastards" of besmirching his reputation, who got Popeye's mother pregnant, married her, and then deserted her. The unlucky daughter of a boardinghouse keeper, his mother was left syphilitic by one husband and penniless by another. And his grandmother was always trying to burn down the boardinghouse with him in it, blaming the burning on the nameless "bastards" who were out to get him (V 296, 299). Popeye did not walk till he was four, had no hair till he was five, had a weak stomach, was impotent, cut up lovebirds and a kitten, and was sent to a home for incorrigibles. Yet is this really an explanation of anything more than the physical fact of Popeye's impotence? Does it explain why he killed the animals or, later, Tommy's dog and Tommy, or why he would want, being impotent, to sexually assault Temple? The explanation is not a series of abstractions, as in the earlier version of Horace, but a series of "facts" that again teases us into interpretation. Far from simplifying Popeye's motivation, the "facts" complicate it, warn us to avoid reducing Popeye to an allegorical symbol.[15] As Faulkner says at one point, Popeye was to him "another lost human being. He became a symbol of evil in modern society only by coincidence but I was still writing about people, not about ideas, not about symbols" (in Gwynn and Blotner, p. 90). Faulkner's addition continues a narrative that never ends because the work of interpretation is never done and the "bastards" remain forever nameless.

II

The final test of an author's text, and of the visions and revisions that produced it, is the power it exerts over us as we read, and in such power few novels excel *Sanctuary*. By placing Temple's story nearer the beginning and continuing it for ten chapters without interruption from her date with Gowan to her rape, Faulkner makes the narrative as breathless and full of fright as Temple herself, running off porches and confronting rats of both species. At which point comes the first great shock, the rape itself, not reported but placed in a horrifying context—among the rats and the gnawed corncobs, with Tommy's dead body outside the door, with the repulsive antagonist inside, all this culminating in the disgusting image of "the old man with the yellow clots for eyes," to whom Temple appeals in vain (V 99). Next follows an easing of the narrative tension (but with heightening suspense) as we shift back to Jefferson and Horace's involvement in the case, only to return obsessively to Temple, raped and

---

[15] See especially O'Donnell, pp. 28–29.

bleeding, too traumatized to escape at Dumfries, then imprisoned at Miss Reba's in a kind of nihilistic suspension of time, symbolized by the clock, while over her cringing body jerks and whimpers and whinnies her sadistic rapist—a scene horrible enough without our yet knowing why Popeye whinnies.

At this point Faulkner's narrative genius is at its best, for he begins to merge our consciousness, our wish to make things right, with Horace's. His and our contempt for the hypocrisy of Christian Jefferson become one, and we embark with him on the same anxious search for Temple, in a sense prodding him, for *we* know where she is. The comic interlude with Virgil and Fonzo at Miss Reba's works precisely because of our concern for Temple and for the form of slavery that brothel represents. Our laughter[16] sets us up for a further and greater shock. We share Horace's compassion and concern—as apparently even Miss Reba does (V 204–5). They both plead with Temple to talk to Horace, to save Ruby's baby's father, and the immobile ridge underneath the covers reminds us of the traumatized Temple's hiding from the doctor and cringing from Popeye the night of the rape. Then something extraordinary happens: after Miss Reba assures Temple of *Popeye's* safety if she testifies, Temple flings the covers back, sits up abruptly, and we confront, along with Horace, a new Temple: "Her head was tousled, her face puffed, two spots of rouge on her cheekbones and her mouth painted into a savage cupid's bow. She stared for an instant at Horace with black antagonism, then she looked away. 'I want a drink,' she said, pulling up the shoulder of her gown" (V 207). Temple has become a gangster's moll, a hollow painted mannequin who tells her story with a kind of "pride" (V 209). Horace's nausea that night is caused in part by his pessimism in the face of such corruption: "Better for her if she were dead tonight, Horace thought, walking on. For me, too. He thought of her, Popeye, the woman, the child, Goodwin, all put into a single chamber, bare, lethal, immediate and profound: a single blotting instant between the indignation and the surprise" (V 213–14). He longs for the obliteration of consciousness itself.

Here again we are invited into Horace's consciousness, to be equally nauseated by the Horror (as Conrad might have put it)—and what is worse, our own complicity in it. For what Horace has discovered, at least subliminally, is that Popeye did to Temple no more than what he desires to do to Little Belle, who stares out of the photograph in such "voluptuous languor, blurring still more, fading, leaving upon his eye a soft and fading aftermath of invitation and voluptuous promise and secret affirmation like a scent itself" (V 216). His double vision of Temple/Little

---

[16]For good treatments of the comic dimension of the novel, see Frazier and Rossky, included herein, and also Miller and Esslinger.

Belle bound naked to a flat car confuses not only the two figures—as well as his own—but images of ingress and egress, penetration and expulsion, orgasm and vomit, with images of womb and tomb, blood and black bile, life-giving sex with the death it inevitably involves. Horace's wish fulfillment is manifold, for it involves thrusting all young girls back into a womb of suspension in "nothingness" and at the same time the life-pulsing "furious uproar of the shucks" with which his own sexual desire—and that of the reader—is inevitably linked.

Immediately, however, by a fine narrative turn, we are granted a respite from negation as we watch Temple apparently try to escape. She bribes her guardian Minnie to let her out for a few minutes, makes a phone call which we are led to believe is to her family, and later frantically breaks away. We find ourselves hoping she will make it to the rendezvous with her rescuer. Our hearts sink when Popeye's car pulls to the curb. Then we are utterly astonished when her words reveal that she was going to meet a rival to Popeye. The very speech patterns indicate that she is radically altered: " 'He's a better man than you are!' Temple said shrilly. 'You're not even a man! He knows it. Who does know it if he dont?' " And incredibly she calls him "daddy" (V 224).

The reader's consciousness has now outstripped Horace's, as stunning revelations flash by at a rapid pace, some of them cryptic. Temple condemns Popeye because he is not a real man. We begin to understand Popeye's posture at the bedside. We wonder what she means by "You couldn't fool me but once" (ibid.). At a dizzying speed of narrative, which imitates the car's speed and Temple's inebriation, we are propelled past her seductive playing with Popeye as she tries to get his gun, past her fantasies about Red's death and the "long shuddering waves of physical desire" that begin to break into our consciousness (V 231), to perhaps the most shocking moment in the novel as she and Red rendezvous in the room:

> He came toward her. She did not move. Her eyes began to grow darker and darker, lifting into her skull above a half moon of white, without focus, with the blank rigidity of a statue's eyes. She began to say Ah-ah-ah-ah in an expiring voice, her body arching slowly backward as though faced by an exquisite torture. When he touched her she sprang like a bow, hurling herself upon him, her mouth gaped and ugly like that of a dying fish as she writhed her loins against him. (V 231–32)

After this shock, the comedy of Red's funeral is macabre indeed, an empty laugh in an empty ritual in an empty cosmos, imaged forth in the six empty Packards that follow Red to his grave. Miss Reba's account of Popeye and Red's perversity is all but anticlimactic: we realize now that Popeye brought in Red to placate Temple's insatiable appetite (V 250), that Popeye, jealous, then forbade them to see each other, while Temple grew as "wild as a young mare" (V 251). By the time of Horace's last shock, as his consciousness catches up with ours, we too are numb and not surprised at Temple's testimony. All the sound and fury recede into the silence of Lee's bonfire, that nonpurgative annihilation of his raped and mutilated body and almost of consciousness itself. The novel winds down its denouement to the perfect desolation of the last triple image: Horace, Popeye, and Temple bored out of existence.

III

I have written so far only of Faulkner's skill. But great skill alone will not make a great novel. The vision of life, too, must be profound, and it is this dimension of *Sanctuary* that the following essays explore. I begin with the best of the sociological interpretations—the mode that dominated criticism in the first several decades—Olga Vickery's reading of the novel's theme as a failure of society to live up to its ideals and a failure of its various codes to protect its members.[17] I proceed next to the best psychological criticism. Dr. Lawrence Kubie's study of the theme of impotence remains a classic of Freudian analysis. In the other psychological essay, T. H. Adamowski, by means of a Sartrean analysis, brilliantly reinterprets Popeye's mechanical appearance as a mask of transcendence.[18]

The next group of articles, those by David Frazier, Aubrey Williams, and William Rossky, pursue various strains of imagery in the novel in order to trace out its profoundest implications of horror, implications that are ultimately metaphysical. Frazier examines imagery that reveals a movement from traditional values to nihilistic modernism; Williams, imagery that reveals a theme of initiation into overwhelming evil; Rossky, imagery that reveals the cosmic dimension of the novel's pessimism— "the universal dream-horror of existence."[19]

The next group contains the best mythopoeic criticism. Before Thomas McHaney no one had really explored the novel's relationship with Eliot's *Wasteland* and Frazer's *Golden Bough*. Now we can see that the corncob is no merely gratuitous, sensationalistic detail invented by a sick mind but an important element of myth, profaned in a black parody of vegetation rites that marks the modern world's loss of myth. David

[17]For some other good sociological criticism, see Thompson, pp. 99–116; Straumann, pp. 129–38; and Brown.
[18]For some other good analyses of character, see Creighton and Mason; for an interesting reading of Temple's "Electra complex," see Cypher.
[19]For other good readings of the metaphysical implications of the novel, see Waggoner, pp. 89–100, and Volpe, pp. 140–51.

Williams, with a neo-Jungian approach, examines the novel in terms of a conflict between the sterile male attitude toward women and sex and the fertile female principle itself, personified in Temple Drake in her destructive phase as she takes unrelenting vengeance on those who have perverted and abstracted sex.[20]

Essays in the last group focus on structuralist concerns: poetics, stylistics, and language. Arthur Kinney's piece, from a book on Faulkner's narrative poetics, examines the way in which the reader must employ his or her "constitutive consciousness" to create meaning out of structural patterns of the narrative. George Toles's piece describes stylistic devices and tropes that contain neither character nor meaning and so leave us with signs that are never quite adequate but point to the empty "space between" observer and observed, signifier and signified. And finally, Philip Weinstein's article examines both the need for and, at least in Temple's case, the failure of verbal sanctuaries that provide a retreat from the chaos of existence, Nietzsche's abyss.[21]

IV

I conclude with Weinstein because his epigram from Nietzsche suggests a further restatement of the meaning and the power of this novel. Malraux once wrote that "*Sanctuary* is the intrusion of Greek tragedy into the detective story" (Warren, p. 274). He means by tragedy the sense of irreparable destiny—and the power to convey it. But *Sanctuary* can perhaps be better illuminated by the light of Nietzsche's *Birth of Tragedy*. The fundamental conflict in the novel can be characterized as that between Dionysiac and Apollonian forces: between the blind, irrational, sexual drive of the life force, impervious to individuals; and the visionary, rational *principium individuationis* of culture and civilization.[22] The Dionysiac is imaged throughout the novel as the deafening cicadas or the writhing honeysuckle or the stifling wistaria or especially the "wild and

[20]For a different approach to the image of women in the novel, see Page, pp. 71–90.

[21]For more traditional stylistic analyses, see especially Reed, pp. 58–73, and Guérard.

[22]Whether Faulkner read Nietzsche is, as far as I know, undetermined, but Nietzsche was certainly in the air, for example in the writings of H. L. Mencken, and Faulkner certainly employs Bacchic imagery in his writing, as in the description of Eula Verner in *The Hamlet* (p. 95) and several passages deleted from the penultimate version of *Sanctuary*. Here is an extraordinary passage, perhaps intended for use in characterizing Horace's response to Little Belle and the grape arbor, but discarded on the back of a carbon sheet of the typescript of *Sanctuary* (my transcription is tentative, and I quote only a portion): "amid the seething bubbles of the waxing grape, had he thot [*sic*] to hear that hard, small clattering flash of heart-shaped hooves where the ravished vine, back-springing, revealed clustered head, mouthward hand, scuttling flank and the cold pale chatter of sparks between spurning hoof and flag" (p. 122ᵛ).

waxlike bleeding" of the grape blossoms (V 13), the force that drives
relentlessly through Little Belle and Temple to madden Horace—and
also as the mindless force of Temple's salmonlike mouth, "gaped and
ugly like that of a dying fish" (V 232). But its power is perhaps best
imaged in a negative figure, that of the deaf, dumb, blind Old Man,
who is no longer symbolic of Wisdom or God but who vegetatively
merely eats and defecates and phototropically moves his chair along the
porch to follow the sun (V 44). Ironically, after she first sees him, Temple
tries to pray but cannot "think of a single designation for the heavenly
father, so she began to say 'My father's a judge; my father's a judge' " (V
50). The most horrifying aspect of the Old Man figure is that, as Temple
again tries to pray at the moment of her rape, she can visualize only him,
can protest only to him. With his "hands crossed on top of the stick" like
those of her father, he has become a Father-Judge-God surrogate who
unheedingly stares out of nothing into nothing with his "yellow clots for
eyes" (V 99). In a manuscript passage Faulkner deleted, Temple, while
being raped, is "thinking of the old man, thinking that this is what he
lives in, as tho [sic] it were a home, a room; then she couldn't see either"
(ms, p. 67). The reference for "this" is at once her womb and the cosmos
itself—a Dionysiac image of the blind, pulsating anonymity and mind-
lessness of the life force, what Nietzsche calls "the Original Mother, who,
constantly creating, finds satisfaction in the turbulent flux of appearances" (p. 102).

The Apollonian in *Sanctuary* is best imaged in Horace, with his Oxford
education, his books, his constant appeal to justice and civilization.
Horace represents the Apollonian gone awry. He is what Nietzsche
describes as Socratic man, he who rationalizes, systematizes, dogma-
tizes, and denies the body; he is the man whom Nietzsche describes as
"enthralled by the Socratic zest for knowledge and . . . persuaded that he
can staunch the eternal wound of being with its help" (p. 108). It almost
seems as if Faulkner had this passage in Nietzsche in mind when he drew
Horace's image of cauterizing consciousness "out of the old and tragic
flank of the world" (V 214)—a world Faulkner earlier describes as
bearing "old wounds" (V 147). Against such a man and the culture he
represents, devoid of living myth and repressive, the Dionysiac impulse
will rebel with a vengeance, as it does memorably in *Sanctuary*.

Perhaps, then, Faulkner's novel approximates tragedy in Nietzsche's
sense in that it forces us to witness the reassertion of the Dionysiac, to
look again into the "original chaos" (V 147) where lurks the truth of
Silenus—"What would be best for you is . . . not to have been born, not
to *be*, to *be nothing*" (Nietzsche, p. 29)—yet at the same time, unlike
Horace, to find sanctuary in art, that grand, tragic illusion of "ordered
chaos" (V 147) which reconvinces us of the value of individual existence.

After all, do we not a half-century after the publication of *Sanctuary* still celebrate the name of an individual who changed the way we see the world—William Faulkner?

Crime and Punishment: *Sanctuary*

by Olga W. Vickery

... Temple's rape and Tommy's murder invoke certain social and legal rituals of justice which are more interested in completing the pattern of crime and punishment than in understanding its moral complexity. Violence is thus countered with violence whether in the form of a legally prescribed and exacted death sentence or a lynching performed by an infuriated mob. It is the act of murder that is being punished and the final grotesque and ironic proof of this is that the wrong man dies, his death satisfying the ritual of justice even as it reveals its ultimate injustice. In the process, Goodwin's self-elected executioners break the law, kill an innocent man, and debase their own moral nature, all in the name of justice and morality.

Even as this pattern crystallizes, Horace Benbow is forced to re-evaluate it in the light of his own growing knowledge about the murder and his moral sense. As a product of his culture and tradition, he begins by assuming that society is the repository of human values and that it will act humanely and rationally even though individuals within it may fail to do so. He ends by uttering some of the bitterest condemnations of Jefferson's moral complacency, hypocrisy, and heartlessness to be found in any of Faulkner's novels. Disillusioned by his society, he yet has faith in the power of truth and the unimpassioned due process of law, but he finds that the court too lends itself to the horrifying travesty of justice based on prejudice and emotional appeals. Even religion proves hollow as the church turns viciously on Ruby while God, whom Horace believed to be "a gentleman," remains genteelly indifferent to the subversion of his divine laws by human ones. What reduces Horace to a state of shock is the discovery not of evil but of the shoddy foundations of his vision of a moral and rational universe, supported and sustained by the institutions of the church, the state, and the law.

All the groups with which Horace comes in contact during his desperate effort to make truth and justice prevail fall short, though in

different ways, of his harmonious vision. Jefferson's respect for law and
social morality manifests itself in self-righteousness and unconscious
hypocrisy while its preoccupation with social values leads to an indifference to personal values. Thus, Ruby is first branded a whore, an
adulteress, and a murderess, and then harried from one shelter to
another in the name of decency and respectability. Horace himself
becomes the subject of gossip and condemnation simply because he
refuses to accept the public judgment of her or to treat her inhumanely.
In contrast to Jefferson's concern with social morality, Goodwin and
Ruby do realize certain personal values in their love for each other, in
their child, and in their care for Tommy and the old blind man.
Similarly, Miss Reba shows a very real if maudlin love for the departed
Mr. Binford and is able to sympathize with Ruby whom she does not
know. On the other hand, both Goodwin's and Miss Reba's households
exist in defiance of law and the rules of society. Each group thus lacks
some quality essential to Horace's ideal of man in society enacting his
own moral nature.

Furthermore, each group, marked by its own distinctive attitude and
code of behavior, is both exclusive and excluded. The result is an uneasy
antagonism flaring into violence whenever a member of one group
intrudes into another. This pattern of intrusion and consequent violence
is presented in its mildest form by the town boys gathering outside the
college to watch the dance. The students become louder and more self-
assertive, while the town boys scrawl lewd remarks about coeds on
lavatory walls and strew the road with broken glass. More central is the
arrival of Popeye at the Old Frenchman place. Indifferent to personal
and social values alike, and therefore as much an intruder at Goodwin's
as he is at Miss Reba's, Popeye by his very presence is a source of latent
violence over which Goodwin manages to maintain a precarious control
until two more intruders, Temple and Gowan, introduce a new and
explosive element into his house.

By attempting to impose their code on a group and in a situation
where that code is not only meaningless but dangerous, Temple and
Gowan generate the violence which overwhelms them. Gowan's adolescent conviction that the honor of a Virginia gentleman is measured by
his ability to drink every man under the table determines his behavior
both with the town boys and later at Goodwin's. For him, the social and
moral criterion is simply one's capacity for liquor. He actually seems to
believe that by outdrinking Van he can establish his own standards of
behavior and hence his control of a situation long since out of hand.
Appropriately, he can only judge the events in which he and Temple
have become involved and his own responsibility for them in terms of
that same sorry code. He thinks not of what might have happened to
Temple but of her returning among people who know him to reveal that

he has committed the "unforgivable sin"—not holding his liquor—which makes him forever an outcast in decent Virginia society. Gowan's abject despair over his folly and his hope that the extent of that folly will never be revealed indicate not so much his youth and stupidity, though that is also present, as his inability either to act or to think in any but the ways established by his group. His obsessive concern with social values has atrophied his every moral and human instinct. In him conformity has been carried to an extreme at once ludicrous and tragic.

Like Gowan, Temple seems to be dominated by campus mores but as they bear upon sex rather than liquor. At seventeen, she already fits easily into the artificiality of campus life, a life of discreet promiscuity and irresponsibility. Thus, while she apportions her favors between the college and the town boys, she herself remains inviolate and unmoved, "her eyes blankly right and left looking, cool, predatory and discreet." (32) But the responses she provokes anticipate those of the men at Goodwin's. Gowan, enraged by Doc, one of the town boys, truculently accuses Temple of denying him while playing "around all week with any badger-trimmed hick that owns a ford." (43) Doc, in his turn, becomes progressively more belligerent with Gowan and more resentful of Temple's retreat as he mimics her constant reminder that her father is a judge. The degree of her promiscuity is not at issue. What is important is that she has sought excitement by arousing desire while reserving the right to retreat into the sanctuary of her family. This pattern is, of course, repeated when the presence of her family in the courtroom enables her to evade moral action, this time at the cost of a human life.

Yet like Gowan, she clings to her customs in the presence of an alien group. Temple can never quite rid herself of the unnatural flirtatiousness and the arch provocativeness which had served her well at Ole Miss because the young men also knew their role in the *pas de deux* of sexual teasing. The men at the Old Frenchman place, however, do not know the rules of her game and have no intention of permitting her to establish them. For them, the only relationship between a man and a woman is sexual; and crude and violent though it may be, it still possesses a vitality and forcefulness which at once repels and attracts Temple.

Caught between her longing for the safety of her own world and her desire to share in the "adventure" of this new one into which she has stumbled, Temple reaches a state of semi-hysteria. She attempts to persuade herself that the two worlds are identical, or if not, that hers has the power of control. Her family, the guardians of public morality, the representatives of the forces of law and order—a judge, two lawyers, and a newspaper man—should certainly be sufficient to intimidate a Goodwin, a Van, or a Popeye. But her wish not to be protected reveals itself in the constant advance and retreat, provocation and cringing withdrawal, that mark her behavior throughout her stay at Goodwin's. She forces

herself on the attention of all the men including Popeye whose callous
aloofness is not easily invaded and whose sexual desires are certainly not
easily aroused. Temple's provocativeness, like Gowan's cavalier use of
the bottle, are natural or at least accepted forms of social behavior in
their world. At Goodwin's they become grotesque in their inappropri-
ateness and highly dangerous once they are translated into the language
of the Old Frenchman place. The flirtatiousness is construed as an open
invitation and the drunkenness as indifference to what may happen.

Time and again Temple is given the opportunity to leave; time and
again Ruby warns her to be quiet, to stop running, to stop impressing
her fear and desire on the men. But she persists, half-fascinated by the
idea of her own rape and half-dreading the actual experience. She can
never quite make up her mind to flee either at Goodwin's, the filling
station, or Miss Reba's. It is not her fear of encountering greater evils or
dangers but her fascination with the idea of violence that holds her
immobile. For only by becoming the victim of violence can she participate in Ruby's world without losing her position in her own. Since she
does not will her rape, but only passively suffers it, she is freed of
responsibility for it, thus enabling her to preserve her social innocence
no matter what physical or moral degradation she experiences. In Ruby's
spare room, her fear almost forgotten in her excitement and anticipation, Temple goes through a self-conscious ritual of preparing for her
victimization and self-sacrifice. She combs her hair, renews her makeup,
glances at her watch repeatedly, and lies down to wait, "her hands
crossed on her breast and her legs straight and close and decorous, like
an effigy on an ancient tomb." (84)

In Temple's later account of the night she spent "in comparative
inviolation," the alternation between fear and desire is obvious. Her wish
to evade the coming rape is expressed by her fantasies: her vision of
herself as somehow physically sealed against contact, as dead, as a
matronly schoolteacher, and finally as an old man with a long white
beard. But this is balanced by her repeated cries of "Touch me! You're a
coward if you dont." And at the very moment of her rape, Temple's
scream is one of mingled protest and exultation: " 'Something is happening to me!' " (122) At last even the naive and inexperienced Horace
realizes that the self-confessed "victim" is "recounting the experience
with actual pride, a sort of naive and impersonal vanity." (259)

At Miss Reba's Temple gives full scope to her inclinations while still
playing the role of "victim-prisoner." The door which she carefully locks
not only keeps Popeye out but herself within. Certainly when she desires
to leave, neither the door nor the servant-wardress stand in her way.
During her stay she becomes completely corrupted, not because she is
kept in a whore house, not even because she has accepted a gangster for a
bed-mate, but because her capacity for moral commitments and re-

sponsibilities has steadily and persistently declined until in the underworld it is wholly atrophied. She has absolutely no interest in Red, her lover, as a human being. At the moment of his greatest danger, her one thought is to obtain just one more second of sexual gratification; and later she does not regret or mourn his death but only that "it will never be again." In short, Temple eagerly abandons all the social values of her group without accepting the personal values which, however minimal, lend significance to the lives of Ruby and Goodwin.

Temple's excursion into the underworld is paralleled by Ruby's forced sojourn in Jefferson. With her practical common sense or suspiciousness, Ruby not only accepts but jealously guards the isolation of her world, " 'asking nothing of anyone except to be let alone, trying to make something out of her life.' " (139) Hence, she furiously resents Temple, the intruder who threatens her security. But she is also aware that she herself is the intruder in Jefferson and calmly accepts its intolerance and cruelty. She moves without protest from the Benbow house to the Hotel to the lean-to shed room in ironic repetition of Temple's flight from room to room at Goodwin's. But even in the shack Ruby is not safe from Narcissa who feels that her world has been threatened by her brother's interest in a woman who is not his kind. Though Narcissa consistently reveals a complete indifference to the moral qualities of any act including her own, she is intensely concerned with the interpretation that may be placed on these acts by people she knows. As she carefully explains to Horace, " 'I dont care where else you go nor what you do. I dont care how many women you have nor who they are. But I cannot have my brother mixed up with a woman people are talking about.' " (220) It is with and through Narcissa that Jefferson rises to protect public morality, to speak in defense of an " 'odorous and omnipotent sanctity' " (221) in the eyes of which Ruby and Goodwin are murderers, adulterers, and polluters of " 'the free Democratico-Protestant atmosphere of Yoknapatawpha county.' " (151)

Narcissa is coolly indifferent to the methods she uses as long as they succeed in bringing her brother, who refuses to conform to Jefferson's preconceptions and prejudgments, back into the fold. She points out that while he has been babbling about truth, justice, and responsibility, he has succeeded in offending social decorum past the point of forgiveness by taking another man's wife and then abandoning her, and finally, by sheltering a "streetwalker," "a murderer's woman" in his apartment. She attempts to frighten him with public opinion, shame him by an appeal to the Benbow past and tradition, bribe him with an offer of a better criminal lawyer than he is for Goodwin's defense, and when all these fail, to disillusion him about Ruby's motives and her needs. Her final step is to deny even lip service to truth and justice: " 'I dont see that it makes any difference who did it. The question is, are you going to stay mixed up with it?' " (221) Horace, of course, refuses to be swayed; but while he is savoring his indignation and exploring the possibilities of action, Narcissa acts expediently and effectively to thwart justice with law and to return a humbled Horace to Belle.

Society, concerned with its own preservation, is thus as intolerant of the saint as of the sinner, of Horace as of Popeye. Strangely enough, there are certain startling similarities between these two morally antithetical figures. Both are primarily spectators rather than participants in life. Popeye's fear of nature, his terror when he senses the swooping owl, is matched by Horace's inability to remember the name of the bird whose call he hears and by his desire to escape from the rich fertility of the land. Moreover, Popeye's rapt and unnatural absorption in watching Temple and Red perform an act in which he can never share is echoed by Horace's painful exclusion from the grape arbor where Little Belle casually experiments with sex. Both are conscious of their isolation and attempt to break out of it, the one through violence, the other through fantasy and hallucination which are themselves a form of violence. Popeye's brutal act fuses with Horace's thoughts and culminates in the nightmare vision of the rape of a composite Temple–Little Belle.

The separation from the world of nature also implies a separation from the nature of man, characterized by a capacity for good and evil. Both Horace and Popeye are therefore incomplete human beings— figures symbolic of good and evil, unintegrated into the human world. Significantly, Popeye is seen only through his actions, violent, reflexive, destructive; in contrast, Horace is all thought, sensitivity, and perception but without the ability to act effectively. The difference between them, and it is, of course, an overwhelming one, is that the latter is isolated by his dream of moral perfection, the former by his total indifference to all moral values. Consequently, they represent two possible aberrations from the social norm represented by Jefferson as well as the two possible alternatives between which society itself must choose. For only by sharing Horace's dream while recognizing it as a dream can society re-examine its conduct and make it once more a living expression of man's aspirations.

Unlike Horace who discovers the force of human relationships even as he is rejected and threatened with lynching by society, Popeye continues to live in complete and utter isolation. The hereditary syphilis and insanity stress his inability to make any kind of meaningful contact, either physical or social, with other people. From his birth he is alone and his survival depends on accentuating that aloneness. The doctor warns that " 'he will never be a man, properly speaking. With care, he will live some time longer.' " (369) Only by eschewing life can Popeye prolong his existence, and only by affirming the reality of death can he, by implication, affirm that existence. His killing the various animals is more than precocious sadism: it is his attempt to gain a fleeting and illusory sense of life through the very act of destroying it. Oddly enough, the same motive is present in his attachment to his half-crazed mother. Since he is rejected by all the groups with which he comes in contact, she is his only link with the human world, the source and therefore the living proof of his own existence.

Into this sterile, circumscribed world of Popeye's, Temple introduces lust, herself desiring that violation of which she suspects Goodwin to be capable and which she later admires so greatly in Red. But all that Popeye can offer is the mechanical violence of a corncob—a horrifying but futile protest against both his impotence and his isolation. His vicarious participation in sex terminated by Temple's revolt, his murder of Red proven an empty gesture, he chooses death out of sheer boredom and the realization that, quite literally, he has never lived. Once having chosen death, he finds it unimportant whether it comes as punishment for killing Tommy, Red, and indirectly Goodwin, or for slaying a policeman in a town he has never visited. It is, after all, the last joke that life will ever play on him and he makes no effort to counter this final gambit.

In contrast to Popeye, Horace wills his own isolation. His desire to escape from Kinston is caused initially by his disillusionment in those relationships which give meaning to a man's life. Experience mocks the poetic ideal as marriage settles into the routine of fetching shrimp from the station and locking doors, and love becomes identified with the grape arbor frequented by a multitude of young men. . . .

But though the beauty he worshipped is denied by experience, Horace yet has faith in goodness. As he travels from Kinston to the Old Frenchman place, Jefferson, the campus of Ole Miss, and finally Miss Reba's whore house, that ideal too is put to the test of reality. For wherever he goes, he carries with him his vision of a world peopled by gentlemen and benevolently ordered by a God who may be " 'foolish at times, but at least He's a gentleman.' " (337) As an ideal, his dream is a noble one; as a description of reality, it is hopelessly inadequate. The crudity of actual life and the intermingling of good and evil in the very texture of experience leave him bewildered and helpless. The very ideals which make him an unerring judge of his society render him incapable of fighting that society.

All of Horace's actions are thus marked by a curious bifocal vision. As he becomes actively involved in helping Goodwin and Ruby, he sees various events and relationships with increasing clarity. But this is dependent on his intuitive comprehension of certain complex situations and their moral quality. Consciously, he cannot help but see through the eyes of a forty-three year old gentleman lawyer, scholar, and poet. He consistently forces the material of his perceptions into a pattern of abstractions which reduce irrationality and complexity to a simple order. He is, in short, hampered by . . . innocence and naive faith in reason . . . Reason and his legal training mediate between Horace's responses and his actions with the result that he finds himself conducting a mock battle with a phantom opponent: armed with Truth, Honor, and Justice, he assails Evil. The battle of abstractions continues while beneath it the intensely human drama of experience is played out to its bitter conclusion.

The source of Horace's frustration is his discovery that his concepts of justice and honor have no coercive power or even influence over either experience or people. When driven to it, Narcissa is prepared to admit that the possibility of a miscarriage of justice is far less important than her position in Jefferson. Senator Snopes and Eustace Graham are concerned only with advancing themselves in the name of justice; both are willing to attribute justice to the side which pays most. Horace cannot even convince Ruby and Goodwin, who have the most to lose, of the importance of truth. Goodwin decides simply to take his chances with the law while Ruby prepares to pay Horace for undertaking Goodwin's defense in the only way she can. The final and complete subversion of Horace's ethical system comes when he sees the Jefferson mob, acting in the name of the very justice he has defended, kill Goodwin.

It is increasingly borne in upon Horace that he will have to stand and act alone. Though for a while he is strengthened by a stubborn courage, he is, nevertheless, doomed to fail. Because he himself is unsure of his ability to take control of a situation, he still relies for support on words and phrases. He offers Goodwin the protection of " 'law, justice, civilization' " (156) against the concrete menace of Popeye's gun, and talks to Ruby about " 'a thing called obstructing justice' " (158) as a counterweight to her concern for her husband's safety. While he talks to Temple about the importance of truth and justice, Miss Reba cuts through his abstract verbiage with " 'They're going to hang him for something he never done. . . . And she wont have nuttin, nobody. And you with diamonds, and her with that poor little kid.' " (256) The sharp contrast between his generalizations and Miss Reba's concrete statement of the human issues is underscored by Miss Jenny, who points out that his moral indignation and championing of the right is purely verbal and that he is spending his time making speeches instead of doing something. Horace's answer is to go off on another tirade in which he threatens to legislate evil out of existence: " 'I'm going to have a law passed making it obligatory upon everyone to shoot any man less than fifty years old that makes, buys, sells or thinks whisky.' " (199) Presumably his statement is intended ironically, but even so it reveals his habit of thought: one additional law will finally either regenerate or frighten men into living in accordance with virtue, decency, and the moral law.

Even though Horace finds that justice no longer lives in the hearts of men, he still retains his faith in the power of truth—if only all the facts are made available, then innocence and guilt, the victim and the murderer will be unmasked. Truth must prove itself independent of and stronger than individual prejudices and distortions. With Ruby's unwilling help he learns of Temple's presence at the Old Frenchman place; with Snopes's information he tracks her down. With dawning horror he realizes, however, that victim though she may be, Temple is also the cause of her victimization. The responsibility for the rape and hence for Tommy's murder is as much Temple's who provoked it as it is Goodwin's who did not act to prevent it or Popeye's who actually committed it. Gowan Stevens is also involved in the guilt, and even Ruby, who anticipated it and yet walked away, is not without blame.

Horrified as he is by his discovery that good and evil do not live in separate compartments, Horace yet risks a final throw of the dice. He presents his facts to the judge and jury and waits confidently for the only possible verdict. In the courthouse, if no other place, justice and truth must be living realities. Yet they are not—he is defeated and not by deliberate, conscious evil but by self-interest and respectability. Horace's collapse is complete and inevitably so. For through most of his conversations with Ruby and Goodwin one refrain had been dominant, that of "Good God. What kind of people have you lived with?" To find that the evil he abhors is in his own backyard, in Narcissa, in his wife and her daughter, in Temple and her respected father-judge, is too much. The enormity of fighting it becomes the impossibility of even challenging it, and Horace who anticipated total victory submits to total defeat. He returns meekly to Belle and the routine of his life with her. Murmuring " 'Night is hard on old people. . . . Something should be done about it. A law,' " (359) he appears to shrink, to lose stature as he stands alone, gazing at the fragments of the Grecian Urn in whose aesthetic and abstract image he had built his life.

The pathos of this scene arises from the fact that Horace's sanctuary, his imaginative world of moral and aesthetic perfection, has been violated and destroyed by his one excursion into the world of concrete experience. For it is only in the verbal universe, whether philosophic, legal, or poetic, that evil can be isolated as the antithesis of good. In experience evil is a necessary condition of existence which cannot be destroyed without destroying life itself. That Horace contemplates such a destruction, though only in fantasy, suggests that he is not yet ready to live in terms of his painfully acquired knowledge of the real world. Because of his search, the separation of justice and law, truth and belief, dream and reality is recognized; but the task of reuniting them, which is the necessary prerequisite to the salvation of man and his society, is beyond his powers.

William Faulkner's *Sanctuary*: An Analysis

by Lawrence S. Kubie

... In the history of the literature of horror it is possible to recognize stages .... From a boy's tales of adventure, with their naive, exultant triumphs over external dangers, to the deep and biological horrors of "Sanctuary" a series could be traced. In this series it would become evident that this constant preoccupation with fear and horror has a direct bodily meaning. The more naive and childlike presentations are all externalized adventure stories with dangerous situations. The more "realistic," adult, and "morbid" stories penetrate below this surface into the instinctual reservoirs out of which terror arises. There is a direct link between the frequent nightmares of childhood and the rarer but equally significant nightmares of adults, and an identical relation between the naive melodrama of a simple frontier civilization and the sophisticated shocker of a "morbid" modern community.

The problem which faces us reaches to the roots of certain complex issues. In the first place it raises the question of the genesis of anxiety; and in the second place the even more perplexing issue of the paradoxical pleasurable utilization of horror (what is technically known as the "erotization of anxiety"). Indeed it is this paradoxical and perverted utilization of anxiety for "pleasure" purposes, rather than the problem of the genesis of anxiety, which constitutes our immediate concern.

The outstanding feature of this ultrasophisticated literature of biological horror is its increasingly frank reference to some form of genital injury. It is not necessary for this reason to assume that all anxiety is genital in its derivation. It is enough to recognize that there is an important interplay of all phantasies of mutilation and contamination between one instinctual battlefield and another; but that since in normal life the genital normally assumes a position of dominance among the instincts, all manifestations of anxiety tend to become focussed in this direction. Whatever the source, however, the outcome is that through all of the books in which horror plays so large a role, the ultimate manifestation of the major horror is through some form of genital injury.

One might expect to find that a great deal of this literature had been written by women, because so frequently in these tales the victims are women, and since in real life the chief form of genital injury of which both sexes are *consciously* fearful is always the fear of rape, and especially of the forcible defloration of a virgin. Surprisingly enough, however, one finds that it is not women who write of defloration and its terrors, but men. Since the state of terror, whatever its apparent nature may be, must have a personal core to start with, this suggests that there must be a basic fear in all men which merely uses the idea of rape as a less distressing substitute. Therefore one examines the men in these tales of rape for evidence of the nature of this basic fear and finds that they tend to an extraordinary degree to be figures who are crippled either in a directly genital sense, or indirectly through some other form of bodily injury. This crippling produces a state of real or psychic impotence.

It is out of just this sense of impotence that there arises one of the most characteristic nightmares of childhood, one in which the child feels helpless in the presence of danger and either runs frantically hither and thither and never escapes, or else is unable to move at all (*cf.* Temple Drake, in "Sanctuary"). Besides that one may place the not infrequent obsessive phantasy of an adult who finds himself bound helplessly while bandits attack the woman he loves. In such a phantasy the bandits execute for the man that which his own fear of impotence makes impossible; but he is freed from the painful acknowledgment of his fear of impotence by making it appear to be the result of external interference and external agents (that is, the bandits who tie him up) rather than the result of his own internal incapacity. (This, as we shall see, takes place either in fearful anticipation or as a reality not once but repeatedly in "Sanctuary.")

It is for this reason, primarily, that we take it to be no accident that the chief villain in the tale of "Sanctuary" is described as totally impotent. This was not a device chosen by chance out of many alternatives, merely to intensify the horror. It was an inevitable choice; because the whole significance of such horror phantasies is linked to the male's constant subterranean struggle with fears of impotence. . . .

The first part of the book is a troubled, and sometimes confused, nightmare, a nightmare which at moments is vivid and gripping, but which occasionally verges on slapstick and burlesque, with somersaults out of hay-lofts, rats that spring in the dark, dim figures that can be smelled in blackness, eyes that gleam in lightless corners, and so on. Yet all of this buffoonery is in subtle harmony with the sardonic and excruciating denouement. For it is the uttermost limits of sour irony that this impudent, tantalizing, and provocative young girl, who had played fast and loose with the men of her own world without ever giving them the gift she kept dangling in front of them, should escape the relatively honest erotic purposes of the healthy members of the band, only to taunt the impotent and tortured figure of Popeye into committing a criminal assault upon her by artificial means.

That Temple invited the assault with her provocative, if unconscious, exhibitionism, is unquestionable. Ruby Goodwin, the mate of the bootlegger, is made to say that if Temple had only stopped running around where they had to look at her all the time it would never have happened, but that Temple wouldn't stay any place—that "she just dashed out one door and in a minute she'd come in from another direction." Horace Benbow noted that Temple told her story with actual pride, "with a naive and impersonal vanity."

Furthermore, in the face of danger, Temple had a momentary hallucination that her body had changed into that of a boy. The rude awakening from this dream, and the shocking rediscovery of her unchanged anatomy gave rise to a secondary phantasy (one which is familiar enough to psychoanalysts in their study of illness, but rarely encountered in literature), in which there was a fusion of the ideas of rape, castration, and death. (*Cf.* the coffin phantasy.) From that moment, Temple behaves as though she herself were dead, and the blind, dead instrument of revenge. But the subtle and confusing thing is that she destroys first, not those who have hurt her, but those who have helped her. She kills the lover that Popeye procures for her. She kills Goodwin, the bootlegger, by giving false testimony against him. She crushes the lawyer who tries to help. It is only indirectly and in the very end that her taunts help to drive Popeye himself into a virtual suicide.

In the story there is no effort to explain why she sacrifices Goodwin, the potent man, to the furies of the mob and saves Popeye, her impotent malefactor. Popeye's disguised presence in the courtroom can hardly account for it. But Temple has by this time become an almost automatic engine of destruction. Perhaps one may venture the speculation that this paradoxical and perverted impulse to revenge herself on those who have not harmed her, but who are essentially normal in their masculinity, fits the whole history of her defiant, rebellious, and provocative attitude towards boys and men. Her career seemed to shape itself out of her hate of her father and her four stalwart brothers. It is almost as though she said, "To be a woman is worse than death or the same as death. Therefore I will take my revenge upon all you men who are really men. I will excite your desires, but I will not satisfy them. I will laugh in the face of your yearnings. I will gloat over you and scorn you as you drink yourselves into impotence. And finally I will be the instrument of your actual bodily destruction."

Throughout the second part of the book battles one good and valiant, but again feeble figure, that of Horace Benbow. He is a well-intentioned but powerless lawyer. He was "given to much talk and not much else"; and he said of himself, "I lack courage—the machinery is all here, but it won't run." Poor Benbow could not even scrub a floor, much less the community whose need for a scrubbing he felt so acutely.

The story of Benbow, like the story of Goodwin, runs through the book as a contrast to the more essential tale of Popeye and Temple. In his forty odd years, Benbow had gradually built up a weak, wide-eyed, but gallant impulse to tilt against the smug and hypocritical forces of society which his sister, Narcissa, represented. In defiance of convention he had married a woman who had had to seek a divorce in order to marry him; and again in defiance of convention he had now left her. In the face of the mounting hostility of the community towards Goodwin, Benbow tried desperately to save him from an unjust conviction. But he was not strong enough to achieve this, and in the end merely accelerated and expedited his death.

Here the tale is a dramatization of the impact between the forces of instinctual evil (which are represented as rising up out of the pits of the underworld through Popeye and Temple) and the forces of an evil and savage conscience, operating through the blind vengefulness of a mis-directed mob. It represents graphically the struggle which in psycho-analytic shorthand is known as the struggle between the Id (the reservoir of instincts) and the Super-ego (the all but blind forces of a conscience whose operation is by no means always rational and clear). Between the two stands this weak and feeble effort at a realistic dealing with life, embodied in the figure of Benbow. He is the weak representative of the much-battered "Ego," that fragment of the personality which is so often ground to pieces in the battle.

Beneath it all one feels the incessant struggle of Benbow against his own impotence and powerlessness. He is unable to defy the women who cramp him on all sides. All adult women seem to thwart him, to manage his life, to force him into channels towards which he has a revulsion. To carry a box of shrimps once a week from the railroad station to his home for all the years of his marriage, loathing the smell of them, hating the drip of them, identifying himself with "the small stinking spots," which left a trail behind him on the sidewalk, constituted his picture of marriage. Far deeper than that lay his incestuous yearnings for his stepdaughter. These tie him up in horror phantasies, in which he sees himself helplessly standing by while his stepdaughter, Little Belle, plays around with other men. In fact it is this which finally drives him from home. And towards the end of the book he is stirred to a dim recognition of his own impulses when her picture is described "as leaving upon his eye a soft and fading aftermath of invitation and voluptuous promise." At this point he becomes nauseated actively, and soon thereafter, giving in to the social pressure which forces him back to the hated protection of his sister, he returns to his wife. In other words, as he becomes conscious of his intolerable and unacceptable impulses, he experiences a direct revulsion of feeling which causes him to be sick, whereupon he gives up his frantic and compulsive rebellion against society.

The only figures in the book who take life in the body with simple, earthy realism, who hate and murder or love and make love whole-heartedly and without reservation, are Goodwin, the moonshiner, and his mate, Ruby. They alone do not think that "all girls are ugly except when they are dressed." They alone do not subscribe to the parable that "Adam paid no attention to Eve until she put on a fig-leaf." They alone are not moved to revulsions of feeling by excrement, by hunger, dirt, and bleeding, or by any of the other natural phenomena of the body's living. They alone have no fear of the body, be it male or female. They recognize Temple's imprudent coquetry in the face of danger, her blind exhibitionism, her invitation of the final disaster. On her Ruby heaps withering scorn for "just playing at it"; yet she is jealous and fearful of Temple's presence because she knows that this tantalizing and provoca-tive coquetry might in the end seduce Goodwin himself. Together they recognize the significance of that "high, delicate head," the "bold, painted mouth and soft chin," the "eyes blankly right and left looking, cool, predatory, and discreet." To them Temple is no innocent victim. They view her realistically. Perhaps that is why Goodwin must be killed, and Ruby cast out by the savage "conscience" of the community.

It may seem to some readers that the author's claim that the book "is a cheap idea, because it was deliberately conceived to make money" would invalidate any effort to study its contents seriously. This we cannot admit. The phantasy still remains as an expression of more forces than those which the author can consciously control. It is only when the nightmare becomes a little too garish, the horrors too gruesome with a touch of the slapstick, that one notes the tongue bulging in the author's cheek. Naive youths who rent a room in a brothel thinking it is a boarding house, the incredible funeral of Red and its solemn, drunken sequel at Reba Rivers's afternoon "tea" party—all make one chuckle a bit—but for the rest the tale stands firmly on its own unconscious sources. We have suggested above that this literature represents the working out in phan-tasy of the problems of impotence in men, meaning by impotence a frailty in all spheres of instinctual striving. In the end, however, this impotence always is seen to have a direct relation to psychosexual potency. It is as though sophisticated and civilized man is conducting a constant struggle against a sense of impending impotence, a struggle which seems to have in it three direct objects of fear, a fear of women, a fear of other men, and a fear of the community and of society in general. All of these three fears are dramatized in this story.

Futhermore, when a man feels unable to achieve some goal towards which he is struggling, he can in his phantasy handle his sense of powerlessness in one of several ways. In the first place he can people the whole world with other impotent figures, spreading his own sense of infirmity to include everyone, and thus reducing his feeling of painful humiliation. Thus we find in "Sanctuary" that every "respectable" man is in one way or another crippled, impotent, or silly. Only the negro who is hung, and the moonshiner who is burned alive, and Red, the dance-hall boy who is shot, are potent. This is true not only of the major figures, such as Popeye and Benbow, but also of such minor figures as Cla'ence Snopes, or the lamed district attorney, or Gowan Stevens.

Or, secondly, he may comfort himself in dreams of the ultimate triumph of the weak over the strong, of the impotent over the potent. Thus, as we have seen, in every line of the book evil and weakness triumph over goodness and strength.

Or he can turn with his rage against the sources of his humiliation and imagine them overwhelmed with disaster. Consequently, all women are made to grovel before men, whether it be Reba Rivers who keeps the brothel; or Ruby Goodwin who, though triumphant and defiant towards others, is ready to lick the boots of her mate; or Narcissa, who is jilted and falls in love with fools like Gowan Stevens; or Temple Drake, whose lean and immature body exists in the book only to taunt and tantalize men with promises which are never fulfilled, until finally the fulfilling of the promise is taken out of her hands and worked upon her with savage and sardonic vengeance by the sinister figure of the impotent Popeye.

Or again the sufferer from a sense of impotence can turn with sour scorn against the whole structure of society, seeing in it nothing but its pettiest aspects, corroding it with irony, taunting it with the failure of every decent effort at restitution or punishment, mockingly embodying all aspirations in the spirit of hypocritical and waspish women like Narcissa.

By all these devices man tries to evade the acknowledgment of his own instinctual helplessness,—yet none of those devices succeed. Just so Popeye, with intolerable suffering, has to bring in a potent male to mate with the woman with whom he himself can have no successful relationship. Here again one sees the actual living out of the primitive horror-ridden phantasy that arises so frequently in the male who is struggling with impotence fears, the fantasy of being helpless and bound while someone else rapes the woman he loves,—a fantasy which appears not only in the actual experiences of Popeye and Temple, but in the constant anxieties of Benbow about his stepdaughter, Belle.

There remains for the poor male only one other way out, one which never works too successfully, but which is always tried—that is, an effort to ridicule and make fun of his own yearnings, and thus to make his own frustrations more bearable. This appears in the book only in the passages of sudden burlesque.

Yet despite all such devices man cannot free himself from the terror and pain of impotence which break through in horror-ridden phantasies. And that is why, in the end, Popeye is so willing to escape, through the hangman's noose, the tyranny of fears which reigns in his heart. It is Popeye who shrieks like a child at a swooping owl, who in a panic shoots a harmless old dog who has sniffed at his leg, who sucks his cigarettes rather than smoking them, who tries to buy with gifts the girl he cannot woo, who is possessive and jealous, who suffers and yearns and wants and whinnies and froths, and all of whose frustrated yearnings turn to hate. And it is Popeye's very figure which is concretely described in the story in words which make it a graphic representation of the phallus whose impotence is the root of the whole tragedy.

And so, at the last, one is left to wonder about the name. Why "Sanctuary" in a tale in which there is no right of sanctuary, where neither impotence nor potency, neither the life of the defiant rebel nor that of the acquiescent conformist, where neither the free play of instinctual expression nor the life which is dominated by a restricting conscience, provides one with any escape from an ultimate state of doom and disaster? Why "Sanctuary" in a tale in which no one triumphs, and everyone fails? Where in such a horror-driven conception of living is "sanctuary" to be found? Perhaps it is not accidental that in the book the only figure who laughs is "Tommy, the feeb," the feeble-minded lad who sets himself to guard Temple and is shot for his pains. He suffers no unhappiness, but laughs even when his pet dog is shot, and undoubtedly would have chuckled over his own demise had he had time to do so. Perhaps here in this cloudy brain is the sanctuary which Faulkner had in mind. For the rest the term is a mockery which says, "There is no escape from anxiety, no escape from horror; therefore let us make of horror a gay tune to dance to and chortle over; let us roll it under our tongues; let us whistle in the dark to prove that we are not afraid; and let us write books about it, tell our friends, and 'hope they will buy it, too.' "

Faulkner's Popeye:
The "Other" As Self

by T. H. Adamowski

In the criticism devoted to Popeye, in Faulkner's *Sanctuary*, there can
be found what is best described as the "electric-light-stamped-tin" syndrome. A typical example comes in this passage from Melvin Backman's
study of Faulkner: "More symbolic than real, he seems deliberately
'modernistic' and unnatural. He is cold and hard like steel, weightless
like aluminum, and depthless like stamped tin."[1] Only the reference to
Faulkner's "electric light" metaphor is missing (p. 4). At first glance
Popeye does appear to be a character reminiscent of many of the
Snopeses, the kind of creation that Scholes and Kellogg call the "type," a
creation referable to "the most general sort of idea, as Everyman is a type
of general humanity; or to a specific non-human entity as Vergil's Fama
represents rumor; or to a mental state, as in Spenser's Despair."[2]

The critical response to Popeye which I have described suggests that he
is intended by Faulkner to serve as a kind of stimulus to arouse in us
associations with the modern waste land. Indeed, the novelist himself
once suggested that an allegorical conception lay behind Popeye, although Faulkner seems not to have been entirely of one mind on this
matter.[3] By associating Popeye with electric lights, rubber knobs, and
stamped tin, Faulkner does, of course, make him appear thing-like and

---

"Faulkner's Popeye: The 'Other' As Self" by T. H. Adamowski. From the *Canadian
Review of American Studies,* 8 (1977), 36–51. Copyright © 1977 by the *Canadian Review of
American Studies.* Reprinted by permission of the publisher.
[1]Melvin Backman, *Faulkner: The Major Years* (Bloomington, 1966), p. 44. See also Cleanth
Brooks, *William Faulkner: The Yoknapatawpha Country* (New Haven, 1963), pp. 120–21 and
Hyatt Waggoner, *William Faulkner: From Jefferson to the World* (Lexington, 1966), pp. 95–96.

[2]Robert Scholes and Robert Kellogg, *The Nature of Narrative* (New York, 1966), p. 204.

[3]William Van O'Connor, in *The Tangled Fire of William Faulkner* (Minneapolis, 1954), p.
57, quotes Faulkner as having said that Popeye was " 'symbolical of evil'." In 1957,
however, Faulkner said that Popeye had become "a symbol of evil in modern society only
by coincidence but I was still writing about people, not about ideas, not about symbols."
See Frederick L. Gwynn and Joseph L. Blotner, eds., *Faulkner in the University: Class
Conferences at the University of Virginia, 1957–58* (New York, 1959), p. 74.

opaque, but this should not lead us to overlook the manner in which Popeye's curious "flatness" serves to make other characters and the reader experience him not as a "type" or as a general symbol of the age but as a self, a center of intentions.

I suggest that Faulkner makes of Popeye an "object" (all opaque and machine-like) which is, at the same time, possessed of an inner life. The consciousness of Popeye is, in other words, present while being absent. The little gangster is conceived in a quasi-theatrical manner—and it is this conception that makes of him a machine-man—for he is a man of gestures and melodrama, encased in a "role" so carefully defined that the man who gestures and acts is never seen, except, as I shall indicate later, on one occasion.

As Cleanth Brooks has observed, much of Popeye's opacity derives from the author's careful "behavioristic" rendering of him. Brooks calls this technique "naked objectivity": "we are not, for example, allowed inside Popeye's mind as he awaits his execution. The scene is vividly rendered: the curious little man methodically crushing out his cigarettes and carefully arranging the butts in a neat line to form a calendar marking the days that have elapsed. But what is going on inside his head? Why is it that he will not summon a lawyer? Has he resolved upon a kind of suicide? Or is it that he simply cannot believe that he is to be hanged?" (p. 119).[4] Brooks makes the important point that Faulkner's stylistic reticence does not pertain only to Popeye and that it includes Temple Drake as well. It is in Popeye, however, that this austere "objectivity" is most carefully maintained. We never see in the accounts of the hoodlum that analysis of inner states which we find, for instance, in the description of Temple in the corncrib. It is also interesting to note that the kinds of questions which Brooks raises would sound odd if they were directed toward Spenser's Despair, I. O. Snopes, or other famous "types."

Popeye is not cast in such a mould, for he seems to be one more in a line of solitary characters in Faulkner's fiction, a line that includes Bayard Sartoris, Quentin Compson, Addie Bundren, Joe Christmas, and Thomas Sutpen. Unlike those characters, however, Popeye is apparently without anguish. It is as if the behavioral report we receive of him precludes any evidence of anxiety in him about his solitude. Those other characters suffer from their solitude, even when their activities lead them into isolation. But Popeye is apparently in easeful coincidence with his solitude. He is what he is and not some other thing; that is to say, he does not experience the attention to alternative forms of being that we find in a

---

[4]Irving Howe has written that it is "perplexing that a writer who excels in works of radical subjectivity should now confine himself to an approach that can only be called behavioristic." *William Faulkner: A Critical Study* (New York, 1962), p. 194.

Christmas or a Quentin Compson. He has no vision of that "something else" which is the occasion for anguish.

Popeye's thing-like character is not far removed from the one-dimensionality of those Sartorises who create the myth of "Sartoris" in Faulkner's first Yoknapatawpha novel. They too were beyond anxiety, insofar as they were no more than a certain quality of panache and daring. Indeed, it was a move away from mere sartorial panache that gave to John Sartoris his "depth." Unlike the Sartoris heir, Bayard, whose torment Faulkner describes in *Sartoris*, Popeye is not provided with an unhappy consciousness for the reason that, like Man in the work of B. F. Skinner, he has no consciousness. He does not brood over his fate like Bayard; nor does he pursue privacy like Addie. Popeye is simply private—as chalk is white. His past (revealed in Chapter 31) is less a burden for him than it is for the critics who must account for the sudden "history" that Faulkner provides, at novel's end, for this modern automaton. Where a Sutpen (for whom the past is a burden) works for his autonomy, Popeye seems almost nonchalantly in control of his world—as Tommy's references to his cavalier tendency to use his "automatic" would suggest. And where a Joe Christmas seems inconsistent or paradoxical in his efforts to avoid being objectified in Negritude, the little "black man" of *Sanctuary* seems to possess the ease and predictability of material nature. One feels that he will reach for that automatic with the rigorous necessity with which falling apples obey the laws of nature.

And yet all of this is not entirely accurate, for we do not "know" Popeye as we know the fall of the apple. And we do not respond to him as we do to the order of things. Instead we experience his aloofness and his solitude as if we were in the presence of a man with an "inside," with, to continue the metaphor, an intentional "core" that is, by definition, indeterminate. Popeye is not a type in the manner, say, of Dickens' Tite Barnacle, for Popeye is a man of the gesture and not of the tic. The scrupulous objectivity of Faulkner's rendering of him includes an element of the melodramatic that serves to create this mystery that we sense in him.

To borrow a notion of Erving Goffman, Popeye seems to be a "performed character": "I have been using the term 'performance' to refer to all the activity of an individual which occurs during a period marked by his continuous presence before a particular set of observers. It will be convenient to label as 'front' that part of the individual's performance which regularly functions in a general and fixed fashion to define the situation for those who observe the performance."[5] The general and fixed function of Popeye's performance is one of creating fascination while at the same time of maintaining indifference. He fascinates other characters and is indifferent toward them. They are the "audience" for this

---

[5]Erving Goffman, *The Presentation of Self in Everyday Life* (New York, 1959), p. 252.

actor. They are our textual proxies. But Popeye's "real" self is not there for them (or us) to see. Nevertheless, if we do not see the man who acts we know he is there insofar as we realize that Popeye *is* an actor. It is in those gestures invested with melodrama that we detect the psychic dimension, the ghost in the machine, of Popeye. The rigorously portrayed mechanical man is actually, in all of that rigor, the tribute paid by the author to the selfness of his creation.

I do not suggest that we look for "another" Popeye than the words of the text offer, only that we look at Popeye without trying first to make him out to be a symbol for our rejection of the mechanical order that we may believe defines our world. Although he seems to be all electric light bulb and stamped tin, these are only at the foreground of the man. The self of Popeye is to be found in a certain structure that includes the "syndrome" mentioned above as well as its relationship to melodrama, gesture, and the problematic past that is sketched out in Chapter 31. Together they suggest that Popeye's armored solitude is offered by Faulkner as a kind of "solution" to Popeye's primary vulnerability. The latter is the dilemma that the child, Popeye, inherits from others—it is the problem he must solve. Chapter 31 describes for us a man who is open to the dangers of life. The adult man-of-the-gesture, the melodramatic type of the modern, is a Popeye who has taken up that vulnerability and "lived it" in such a way as (almost) to overcome it. Later I will discuss this solution by reference to certain notions of Sartre, whose work is rich in concern with the manner in which we adopt roles in order to resolve the difficulties of a life in a world we must share with other people.

II

For most of the novel Popeye's life unrolls before us in the present tense, and yet Faulkner does devote part of one chapter to Popeye's past. He seems, for once, to be trying to get close to Popeye and to be attempting an "explanation" of the Memphis gangster. The chapter has been the object of much attention from critics, and before we proceed further it is important to see just how it makes sense of Popeye—if, in fact, it does at all.

In the final chapter we learn of the economic hardships posed for Popeye's mother by the flight of her husband and of the "care" the child received from a demented grandmother. The departed father transmitted, it seems, a congenital disease to the child. We learn that Popeye was abnormally slow in developing, that "he did not learn to walk and talk until he was about four years old" (p. 296). By age five he was "an undersized, weak child with a stomach so delicate that the slightest deviation from a strict regimen fixed for him by the doctor would throw him into convulsions." The physician says that alcohol would kill him like strychnine and that " 'he will never be a man properly speaking. With care, he will live some time longer. But he will never be any older than he is now' " (p. 300). All of this in a chapter that shows us a Popeye who, for no apparent reason, allows himself to be condemned to death for a murder he did not commit. If one reads the chapter one is likely to agree with the physician, that Popeye would remain, mentally, a five-year-old.

I do not think, however, that this account of Popeye's past reduces his character, as we see it in the first part of the novel, to a somatic dimension. These are the "facts" with which Popeye must live (as Joe Christmas must live the facts of his racial "inheritance"), but they do not determine his life. Indeed, the chapter contains one striking contradiction of the facts of the adult's character. This is precisely that matter of Popeye's intelligence, or lack of it ("he will never be any older than he is now"), and it calls into question the value of the chapter as an explanation of the whole man. After all, Popeye is quite intelligent—everything suggests this, unless one assumes that evil actions and high intelligence are mutually exclusive of one another. The Memphis lawyer who comes to Popeye's cell is, for example, bewildered by Popeye's indifference to his situation:

> "Are you just going to lie here and let—"
> "I'm all right," Popeye said. "I didn't send for you. Keep your nose out."
> "Do you want to hang? Is that it? Are you trying to commit suicide? Are you so tried of dragging down Jack that . . . You, the *smartest*—"
> (p. 306, emphasis mine)

The lawyer remains in "baffled and raging unbelief," and says that " 'they won't believe it'," in Memphis, when they learn that Popeye has allowed a small-time justice of the peace to hang him.

And surely the lawyer's bafflement is justified, for Popeye is a legendary figure in the underworld. No, the doctor's assessment of his intelligence was wrong. Even Miss Reba attests to Popeye's cleverness, telling Temple that " 'they ain't going to catch Popeye, honey. Smart as he is' " (p. 206). His acceptance of death is not, then, an effect of a certain retardation of the brain. It is better understood as indifference, something reminiscent of that indifference toward death that one finds in the Meursault of *L'Etranger*, including the rejection by each man of the cleric who comes to speak to them of meaning. Mental age is not at issue. Nor are syphilitics necessarily doomed to evil.

But Popeye goes beyond the physician's saying in other ways. The delicacy of his stomach pertains only to its tolerance for alcohol. He is not squeamish about violent stimulations of a moral or psychological kind. It is hilarious to think of this character, who engages in some of the grossest behavior in modern fiction, as suffering from a weak stomach! And while he may not be a man "properly speaking," he is one improperly speaking. He does not give up on Eros because of the tyranny of a useless genital. Not only has he lived longer than the physician expected, he actually appears (as Brooks seems to suggest) to have chosen the time of his death. If the facts of Popeye's childhood are there in order to allow us to see the criminal as a product of his environment (as Irving Howe would seem to imply, p. 197) then they do not succeed. Popeye's past does not coincide with his later life: it exists both in contradiction and in ironic relation to that later life.

Some critics have leaned heavily on the "symbolic" meaning of Popeye's inherited disease in an effort to integrate the last chapter into the novel. Backman, for example, sees in Popeye the "defective product of a loveless syphilitic union[;] he is apart from and against nature" (p. 44). In this reading, Popeye is "forced by impotence into perversion and knowing neither compassion nor morality he personifies a vicious mechanistic destructiveness that is ultimately suicidal" (p. 45). The recourse to madness and the condition of the cerebral tissues is also taken by Olga Vickery. She sees in Popeye's "hereditary syphilis and insanity" a stress on his "inability to make any kind of meaningful contact with other people."[6] Of course Popeye's "contact" with Temple is all too "meaningful."

It is true that Popeye is immoral, lacking in compassion, isolated, and "against nature." In his opacity he seems mechanical.[7] But impotence implies nothing about one's predilection for perversity—one might expect that most perverts are "potent." Nor is there any necessary relationship between congenital syphilis and these other vices of Popeye. Faulkner's symbolism is generally more complex (and compassionate) than these equations suggest. Syphilis cannot be used selectively. Either it "explains" all of Popeye or it explains nothing, and we must understand its true relevance in another way. The mediations that would bind Popeye's behavior to his soma are lacking, and his behavior does not stand in relation to his illness as a bicycle chain's turning to the movement of pedals and gears. One need only recall how carefully Faulkner ties the behavior of Benjy Compson or Ike Snopes to idiocy in order to see how loosely textured the word "insanity" is when applied to Popeye. As Michel Foucault has observed, we tend too often to use "insanity" as a substitute for understanding the meaning of strange behavior: "In our

[6]Olga Vickery, *The Novels of William Faulkner: A Critical Interpretation* (Baton Rogue, 1964), pp. 110–11. [Reprinted above.—Ed.]

[7]In *Quest for Failure* (Ithaca, 1960), p. 211, Walter J. Slatoff refers to Popeye's "complete opaqueness." Slatoff distinguishes Popeye's "environment"—which he believes has little to do with "his problems"—from his heredity, and he argues that Popeye's "problems are entirely pathological."

era, the experience of madness remains silent in the composure of a knowledge which, knowing too much about madness, forgets it."[8]

Another critic, Edmond Volpe, is quite right to remind us that the ultimate responsibility for Popeye's evil goes beyond "the syphilitic father and his demented grandmother."[9] Although I can assent to Volpe's refusal to blame Popeye's evil on his forebears, I think he is wrong to see in the final chapter a link between "human and cosmic evil," with Popeye as a "victim of blind cruel fate" (p. 150). Frankly, I just do not know what "cosmic evil" means in this connection. Hurricanes? "Something" very bad? Volpe sees in Popeye's isolation from the natural and human worlds the sign that he is "outside the circle of the corrupt human fraternity," and that this is evidence of his link to the cosmic (p. 149). But he cannot have it both ways: either Popeye is beyond his father's legacy or he is the victim of a "blind fate" that can only be manifested in his very inheritance from his father of syphilis. We see no fate at work when Popeye stalks Temple. Only a rapist.

We understand Popeye's solitude by seeing his radical "otherness." The behavioral account of him confronts us with the dilemma of "other minds" that the philosophers face when they try to show that we can infer a mind from the body that is all with which we are presented by the Other. Volpe implies this dilemma in his bewilderment over what Popeye is thinking (p. 150)—as did Brooks. Like most novelists Faulkner generally avoids the philosopher's problem by taking the kind of short-cut Alexander took when faced by the Gordian knot: he simply *reveals* the inner life of his characters. Quentin Compson thinks and his thoughts are there before us, on the page. But Popeye only behaves. In the jargon of the philosopher he is "transcendent," and the final chapter ratifies his apartness through its failure to explain him by reference to those levelling pieties of nature and nurture. As we shall see, a psychic dimension is suggested for Popeye, and the data of the final chapter become relevant insofar as they are merely the "facts" that Popeye modifies by his life.

III

Popeye, the adult, at once refuses and realizes his past. The past that Faulkner posits for him is sur-passed to the extent that it leaves him as a question mark for us. The future that seems to be sketched out in advance for him by the givens of his childhood is that of a poor victim of

[8]Michel Foucault, *Madness and Civilization: A History of Insanity in the Age of Reason* (New York, 1967), p. xi.
[9]*A Reader's Guide to William Faulkner* (New York, 1964), p. 150.

social misfortune. He has no rights: to success, to women, to autonomy, to intelligence. As the child of a physician's "strict regimen," he ought to be everyone's object: an open book before the all-knowing gaze of the world. In manhood, however, the formula is reversed: everyone is Popeye's "object," and no one can read him. One might almost say that if there are any "types" in this novel they are to be found among all those characters whom Popeye treats "alike." It is they who are the objects for his contemptuous glance, and they who serve as the instruments for the affirmation of his sovereign indifference. This "victim" victimizes, thus affirming what Sartre has called the "irreductibility of the cultural order to the natural order" and, let it be added, to the social order as well.[10] This reversal of terms, this "irreductibility," is the sign of Popeye's freedom from the past; but his freedom is no random and meaningless activity, and thus it is colored by the past.

The contradictory scandal of a condemned child who becomes a lord of the underworld is Popeye in his solitude. This man who was once a transparent child works hard at effecting opacity in his adulthood. The problematic relation between that final chapter and the rest of the novel is the evidence of Popeye's existential "project"; "a flight and a leap ahead, at once a refusal and a realization, the project retains and unveils the surpassed reality which is refused by the very movement which surpassed it" (*PM*, p. 92). We know of that project insofar as we know of Popeye's past and of its problematic relationship to his adult life. Although he is more than what nature and nurture had "intended" him to be, they are not obliterated by the project that upset their design for his life. And where Popeye finally does show a weakness in *Sanctuary*, becoming once again transparent, it is in his fall from the gestural order of melodramatic solitude to the actions of a man deprived of his sexuality by the contingencies of his birth. At the gestural level is the man who is fascinating to others; at the level of weakness and contingency we see the man who is obscene.

"Fascination is transcendence," Sartre writes, and he argues that it is one aim of fascination to achieve a kind of "seduction" by appearing to go beyond norms and conventional expectations: "By seduction I aim at constituting myself as a fullness of being and at making myself *recognized as such*."[11] In fascination the seducer aims at leading us apart from the everyday world by his gestures, that is by actions performed *for their own sake*. These "self-referential actions" cause us to turn our attention entirely on him. Through them he becomes the man apart: a Christmas-

---

[10] Jean-Paul Sartre, *The Problem of Method*, trans. Hazel E. Barnes (London, 1963), p. 152. Subsequent references in the text to this work are to *PM*.

[11] Sartre, *Being and Nothingness*, trans. Hazel E. Barnes (London, 1957), p. 372. Subsequent references are to *BN*.

as-nigger before fascinated white women, or a sister and brother cast into the hell of the incestuous by a self-fascinated Quentin Compson. Fascination and gesture are important elements of Faulkner's work, and they do not make their only appearance in *Sanctuary*.[12] In these other instances, however, we are involved in the inner turmoil of the self-as-subject. Irving Howe has written that it is perplexing to see Faulkner, a novelist of subjectivity, abandon this concern in his "objective" portrayal of Popeye. Perhaps it is in order, then, to speak of a different concern with subjectivity in *Sanctuary*, a concern with the subject-as-object.

Popeye is closed to us, and we do not experience the restlessness of the interior. Instead we see only that "depth of objective and hidden being" that is all that is available to the fascinated (*BN*, p. 372). We are left, along with the characters of the novel, at the mercy of Popeye. They fear his gun, and we, as readers, try to "figure him out" by reference to nightmarish disease and to the cosmos itself. Because of the absence of the inner record we are not presented with the intentional structure of fascination but only with the *fait accompli*.

Thus, when Sartre describes the intention-to-fascinate, we must eliminate the subjective aim of the seducer and see only the effect that is achieved by his behavior: "I try [in seduction] to constitute myself as an infinity of depth, [and] to identify myself with the world" (*BN*, p. 372). What Sartre means is that the man who fascinates seeks to make us experience him as someone who has access to realms of meaning ("being," in Sartre's idiom) that are closed to us. He tries to make us feel that the possibilities of the world come to us across him: "I manifest by my acts infinitely varied examples of my power over the world (money, position, 'connection,' etc.)" (*BN*, p. 372). The other person will be no more than a captivated subjectivity, in bondage to a freedom (the seducer's) that has hidden itself behind, let us say, certain "fascinating accoutrements of power: limousines, credit-cards, an entourage, etc. What must *not* appear is the vulnerability of the seducer's freedom. It is that freedom, that subjectivity, which is "in hiding" behind the instruments of the seduction.

If we accept Sartre's account (one that I have had to simplify here), such a man is a self locked in on itself. It is a self that has shut the door to the reciprocity (the recognition of mutual freedom) that is the death of fascination. Reciprocity implies that we are in the same world—in Sartre's terms it is the recognition that we must encounter the free glance of each other and not seek to hide that free (and vulnerable) glance behind the wall of fascination. (We recall that Popeye's eye are the color of stagnant water.) Or, to turn to Sartre's account of "indifference," the

---

[12]See T. H. Adamowski, "Joe Christmas: The Tyranny of Childhood," *Novel*, 4 (1971), 240–51.

fascinating self has a "kind of blindness with respect to others." He does not see them as people but as instruments—sexual, political, economic, etc.: "I scarcely notice [others]; I act as if I were alone in the world. I brush against 'people' as I brush against a wall; I avoid them as I avoid obstacles. Their freedom-as-object is for me only their 'coefficient of adversity.' I do not even imagine that they can look at me" (*BN*, p. 380). In Sartre's argument the failure to sustain fascination (remaining an opaque object for others) may lead one to adopt "indifference," but I do not wish to assimilate Popeye into the dialectic of Sartre's argument; rather I would suggest that due to Faulkner's refusal to show us an inner life for the gangster we experience him as both fascinating and indifferent. The Others are fascinated, and he is indifferent to them—his indifference is the occasion of their fascination.

Popeye's first appearance in the novel is evidence of this dual capacity. He always acts in ways that upset normal (or conventionally abnormal) styles of behavior. The man of the "vicious depthless quality of stamped tin" reduces Horace to helpless passivity before him. Popeye "squatted, facing [Horace] across the spring. That was about four o'clock on an afternoon in May. They squatted so, facing one another across the spring, for two hours" (p. 5). There has been no overtly threatening behavior on the part of Popeye, unless it be that he is the essence of threat; but Horace follows him to the Old Frenchman's place as though it were in the natural course of events. The situation is patently fantastic: they sit by the spring, looking at each other, for two hours! In his first encounter with another character Popeye creates not only antagonism but paralysis. In his black suit, with a cigarette dangling from his lips, he is a creature of pure melodrama, a study in the possibilities of gesture. (One thinks of Bogart in *The Petrified Forest*.) Furthermore his "conversation" is baffling. When Horace tells Popeye that he has a book in his pocket, the strange little man asks, " 'Do you read books?' " (p. 4). His very face suggests his transcendence of the ordinary: "the cigarette wreathed its faint plume across Popeye's face, one side of his face squinted against the smoke like a mask carved into two simultaneous expressions" (pp. 4–5).

This encounter establishes that Popeye is beyond the commonplace. Consider his response to Horace's suggestion that they take a shortcut: " 'Through all them trees?' " he asks. Or his remarkable response to the sudden flight of a bird: "with Popeye crouching against [Horace], clawing at his pocket and hissing through his teeth like a cat" (p. 7). These responses are anti-responses. They seal Popeye off from us and reveal his basically contradictory character: the victim-victimizing is also the terrified-terrifying. His very fears color the world with his dark nature. At this point Horace does not consider Popeye as a frightened little man. He thinks of him as being horribly thing-like and unhuman: "he smells

black, Benbow thought; he smells like that black stuff that ran out of
Bovary's mouth and down her bridal veil when they raised her head" (p.
7). Nor is Horace's response a sign that he is *merely* frightened. In
Sanctuary, before Popeye, the quality of fright resembles that of a cobra
frozen by the movements of a mongoose.

Much of the novel's mystery comes not only from the suspense
generated by its plot but also from the mystery that is Popeye himself.
Horace's feelings about the effect of the gangster's presence add to the
quality that Popeye shares with that "black stuff that ran out of Bovary's
mouth": "he was thinking of the first time he saw [Ruby's baby], lying in
a wooden box behind the stove in that ruined house twenty miles from
town; of Popeye's black presence upon the house like the shadow of
something no larger than a match falling monstrous and portentous
upon something else otherwise familiar and everyday and twenty times its
size . . ." (p. 116). The presence of Popeye is the antithesis of the familiar,
and he is able to dominate a world that is much more than he himself—
in some "everyday" incarnation—could ever be. His presence in "black
and nameless threat" marks his unknowability. He is as impalpable and
yet as real as a shadow, a man at the margin of humanity. The unfor-
tunate Tommy describes in amused bewilderment how Popeye once
shot a dog that had sniffed at his heels (p. 19). Tommy's interpretation of
Popeye as the "skeeriest durn white man I ever see" does not make
Popeye into that vulnerable creature described by the physician. Like so
much in Popeye's character, this very trait, in its excessiveness, demands
to be understood; and it must be understood by reference to that balance
of contradictions that makes up the character of Popeye.

Faulkner repeatedly presents him in a manner that emphasizes his
indifferent detachment from others. At times it seems as if the only
illumination we receive on him comes from his matches: "Popeye came
out the door. He lit a cigarette. Tommy watched his face flare out
between his hands, his cheeks sucking . . ." (p. 66). When Temple is taken
from the tavern prior to Red's murder, she is driven past a parked car:
"when they passed it Temple saw, leaning to a cupped match, Popeye's
delicate hooked profile beneath the slanted hat as he lit the cigarette. The
match flipped outward like a dying star in miniature, sucked with the
profile into darkness by the rush of their passing" (p. 234). The matches
serve to cast light only on his threatening quality. In the fashion of
melodrama such episodes mark the world as threatening insofar as
Popeye is at the foreground of the world. As Sartre points out, the person
who fascinates keeps others at a distance from him: "the condition
necessary for the existence of fascination is that the object be raised in
absolute relief on a background of emptiness . . ." (*BN*, p. 177). It is as if
the world, in its multiplicity of everyday details, is absorbed into the
being of the seducer. Others, Van and Red for example, have their

menacing qualities "diluted" by their share in the everyday: Van is a drunk and a lecher; Red gambles and shoots off his mouth. But Popeye is other than the everyday and congruent with the hidden gun that he carries: " 'You could feel the pistol on him just like you knew he had a navel'," Benbow remarks. " 'He wouldn't drink, because he said it made him sick to his stomach like a dog; he wouldn't stay and talk with us; he wouldn't do anything; just lurking about, smoking his cigarettes, like a sullen and sick child' " (p. 105). But this is a child of nightmare, and his response to alcohol is not merely a sign of a chemical imbalance but is part of the total structure of his separation from the world of mere moonshiners, drunkards, and teetotalers. That structure of separation is his character. In other words, a syphilitic flaw has become Popeye's "distinction."

People associate him with danger as one associates it with the skull on a bottle of poison. His very indifference suggests his capacity for violence. Gowan, for example, warns him that he resents Popeye calling Temple a whore: "Popeye turned his head and looked at Gowan. Then he quit looking at him . . ." (pp. 48–49). Temple then takes up the matter until Gowan asks, " 'Do you want him to slam your head off?' " Two movements of Popeye's head are sufficient to intimidate Gowan. The eerie indifference of "then he quit looking at him" tells Gowan what he needs to know. The awe in which people stand of Popeye marks his success in suggesting that he is unsurpassable. Because of his respect for Popeye as a "crack shot" Goodwin prefers to risk conviction rather than to implicate Popeye in the crime: " 'I've seen him light matches with a pistol at twenty feet' " (p. 128). Such gestures warn others to keep their distance, and they certify that the gesturer belongs to another order of being. In the eyes of those who behold these gestures, Popeye is simply a certain number of manifestations of criminal power, of mana.

The man whom we see in Memphis is no less opaque (i.e., in his appearance of pure criminality) than he is at the Old Frenchman's place, but there Popeye is revealed as a man who is attractive to women. When Reba congratulates Temple on her new beau, she tells her that " 'every girl in the district has been trying to get him' " and that one, " 'a little married woman'," had offered Minnie " 'twenty-five dollars just to get him into the room, that's all' " (p. 141). Popeye's aloofness effects other forms of fascination, then, than those of paralyzed fright. In his use of it a sexual deficiency has become a solid asset, making of the man who would never be a man an erotic object.

It is necessary now to qualify what I have been saying about the thing-like opacity of Popeye, his intimidating lack of an "inside," his exterior of pure evil. His capacity to fascinate others comes from this: that one may see in him not only the "precision of a finely perfected machine," but also the "perfect unpredictability of the psychic" (*BN*, p. 400). If we feel him as the essence of threat (as Gowan does when he watches Popeye's head turn) we do not, on the other hand, know that he will necessarily carry out that threat. The suggestion of a "psychic" or intentional dimension for the "mechanical man" is to be found in the uncertainty of the others before the almost machine-like swivel of the head. It is in the responses that others make to Popeye that we sense his self-hood. By radically eliminating any account of an interior dimension from his characterization of Popeye, Faulkner has suggested its presence all the more by relocating it, so to speak, "in" the fear and trembling of Popeye's audience. It is they, the people who have not been deprived of an interior, who signal us that Popeye is more than the sum of his "behaviors."

In fact this relation between Popeye and his audience points to a quasi aesthetic aspect in Faulkner's characterization of Popeye. His acts are gestures in that they are perfectly appropriate to his essence, threat. We experience that essence through those gestures.[13] There is in Popeye a kind of grace. Recall that "delicate hooked profile" as it is revealed in match-light. In his essence (suggestive of a kind of "determinism" that follows from the "laws of violence") and in his indifference (suggestive of a capricious freedom), we find that "moving image of necessity and of freedom . . . which strictly speaking, constitutes grace" (*BN*, p. 400). The others at the old farm preserve a distance from Popeye because they recognize that they may fall prey to the whims of this hidden consciousness that seems to be organized for destruction: "but the purpose of organization may be to terrify. The beauty of the criminal is the perfect organization of Evil, its plenitude, its perfect visibility, its power, its staggering evidence. Beauty can be perfection in ugliness."[14] Or, as Horace puts it, one could feel the gun on him.

Another example of this fascinating beauty is found in Popeye's capacity for what might be called sudden materialization. There is, for instance, the manner of his appearance to Temple as she hides in the corncrib. He moves toward her *in* and *through* silence (p. 99), leading the girl to realize that she is a participant in necessity. "Something is going to happen to me," she thinks. It is a kind of "role" that is being forced on her, with Popeye as director and leading man. On one occasion she

---

[13]"Especially in seduction language [including the language of gesture] does not aim at giving to be known but at causing to experience," *Being and Nothingness*, p. 373. Popeye, and *Sanctuary* in general, share in what Peter Brooks reminds us are the classical connotations of melodrama: "extravagant expression, moral polarization, emotional hyperbole, [and] extreme states of being." See "The Melodramatic Imagination," *PR*, 39 (1972), 205. It is as the embodiment of an "extreme state of being" that we experience Popeye, and in the wake of this experience come the moral and emotional excesses that define his relationship with others.

[14]Sartre, *Saint Genet: Actor and Martyr*, trans. Bernard Frechtman (New York, 1963), p. 98.

leaves the brothel, and a "car, moving slowly along the curb," suddenly appears next to her: Popeye is at the wheel. "Without any apparent movement from him the door swung open. He made no movement, spoke no word. He just sat there, the straw hat planted a little aside" (p. 223). She enters the car, seeing, presumably, in the melodramatic figure of gesture, the sign of power over her world. When he drives away, it is with his characteristic indifference: "with the other hand he whipped the car in and out of traffic, bearing down upon other cars until they slewed aside with brakes squealing, shooting recklessly across intersections. Once a policeman shouted at them but he did not even look around" (p. 225). The final "but" signifies the indifferent transcendence of the mere "others" whom he must "brush against" in the world. There is even a certain beauty in the elegantly melodramatic transition from Chapter 24 to Chapter 25. In the former Red blasphemes and calls Popeye that "dopey bastard" (in certain respects an accurate description). The next chapter opens on Red's funeral. Indeed, Popeye's spirit lingers in the courtroom after the machine-man has left the area. Cleanth Brooks raises the question of why Temple perjured herself at the trial, and he concludes that "Faulkner leaves the answer for the reader to infer" (p. 126). But given her odd account, to Horace, of the rape ("recounting the experience with actual pride") one may hazard the inference that she remains under the spell of the rapist when she refuses to implicate him.[15]

If Popeye reminds us of a machine (the stamped tin syndrome), one must suspect, nevertheless, that there is a "ghost" in it and that "intentions" sustain the gestures of the Actor, intentions that are there, in the text, in the responses of others to those gestures. As a being of gesture Popeye evades the handles that we might be reaching out to place on him, handles taken from the final chapter or from some simplistic analogy to "machine" civilization. That final chapter supplies us with what Popeye is *not* as well as that which he has gone beyond. When he asks the hangman to fix his hair it is one more gesture, one more opaque manifestation of the "psychopathic." But this is the opacity of fascination and not of stamped tin. We remain in fascinated ignorance because those last words of Popeye are a parody of the "last words" of the condemned, a ritual to which Popeye is indifferent. Such gestures are the signs of Popeye's freedom from the "material world" and the circuit of pathology that it had seemed, during his childhood, to outline for him.

But there is a "leak" in this closed gestural "system." By means of his calculated indifference—that is to say, his systematic indifference—

[15]It should be noted, however, that Brooks offers a very elaborate discussion of Temple's behavior in the courtroom, and he concludes that "Faulkner leaves the answer [to the question of why she behaves as she does] for the reader to infer, but everything . . . suggests that . . . she was willing to carry out Popeye's command" (p. 126).

Popeye had gone beyond the limitations of his body and become a fascinating object (a contradiction in terms) to others. Sartre, paraphrasing Hegel, says that transcendence "preserves what it rejects" (*Saint Genet*, p. 231). Like a dancer, whose gestures keep before us the heaviness of a body that is at the same time a delicate lightness, Popeye had transformed smallness, constitutional delicacy, and sexual impotence into assets. They remain always before us, but suspended in the very movement that denies them. They were the limitations on Popeye's power to act (rather than to gesture): to be big, tough, and sexual. But the gun, the corncob, the black suit, the cigarettes, the violent stimulants of rape and murder—all these "props" had coalesced in the melodrama of gesture to make him into an act-or: The Actor. The leak in this system comes when Popeye leaves the stage. It is not in the final chapter that we find it, but in what we learn of Popeye from Miss Reba and her guests after Red's funeral. The "flat" Popeye of the performance disappears, and, for a brief moment, we see the harried *man* who performs, in all of his impotence and frenzy.

In his remarkable bedside manner Popeye becomes a species of what Sartre calls the "obscene": "the obscene appears when the body adopts postures which entirely strip it of its acts and which reveal the inertia of its flesh" (*BN*, p. 400). As an example of this obscenity, Sartre cites "certain involuntary waddlings of the rump." The naked body tries to walk in grace, but the "rump is like an isolated cushion which is carried by the legs," obedient to the laws of weight (*BN*, p. 401). The gesture, recall, is an action performed for its own sake—as when a nightclub singer pauses in mid-song to light a cigarette and to set a mood. But the obscene is a failed action. The transformation of Popeye does not occur during that cob rape which we might, at first, suspect to be the privileged space of obscenity in the novel. That famous episode is never shown to us. Popeye materializes in the corncrib; we learn of Temple's anxiety, and then we see her bleeding in the car. The cob rapist is still the Actor and the Prince of Evil. We do not see him push his "tool," hear him moan, or see him in any way suffer from the limitations of the cob as a substitute phallus. In Temple's report to Horace there is only the eeriness of Popeye and of his "nasty little cold hand," "like alive ice" (p. 211). The episode is shaped by her fantasy of becoming a corpse and a boy. In a curious way the cob rape has come to stand for the fascination of Popeye—as one knows if one has ever taught the novel and overheard the informal conversations of students concerning this episode.

When we learn of Popeye's use of Red in the brothel, however, we are given not the grand being of the gesture but that little man who is all inadequate flesh. One of Reba's guests tries to decipher him, and she suggests that " 'maybe he went off and got fixed up with one of these glands, these monkey-glands, and it quit on him' " (p. 250). Suddenly he becomes a kind of freak, and he threatens to give the house a bad name (people might call it a "French joint"). Reba says, " 'Yes, sir, Minnie said the two of them would be nekked as two snakes, and Popeye hanging over the foot of the bed without even his hat off, making a kind of whinnying sound' " (p. 251). "Without even his hat off"—this pathetic lapse of a man who was in a hurry, combined with the escape of desire in a "whinny" transform the Popeye who is transcendent into a dependent creature of weakness. Now others *know* him. Minnie has peeked through a keyhole and told all. In the language of Sartre, Popeye has become a "transcendence-transcended," and we see in his moment of obscenity the "inertia of [his] flesh." We know of the limp object that hangs from his groin and that had always been veiled by his gestures. Like every Actor he had been dependent on the gaze of Others, but he had controlled what they saw by giving to them only the performance. Now he falls beneath an unperceived glance. He leaves the open world of the "theater" where he had gestured, for the closed world of a brothel's bedroom—where he fails to act, insofar as he acts by proxy. There in the dark it was action, not gesture, that the gangster had intended. But all we see, through the eyes of a maid (*our* proxy), is his shame.[16]

Does this moment of Popeye's behavior validate the claim that he is merely at the intersection of nature and nurture? Certainly, for a moment, these seem to claim him. But if we learn that Popeye is limited by his disease (in sexual intercourse he requires a proxy), we have known this in generality already. This episode is merely one more ironic denial of his past (he can make love after all: on his terms!) which, like all the others, assumes its brutal existence. This scene differs from them, on the other hand, in that it registers only the effort of his life and the terrible gap that has been erected between a public and a private man.

His syphilis is not the key to an understanding of Popeye. He may be a syphilitic but not all syphilitics are Popeye. The "existential" meaning of this character is that he lives his disease in a certain way: above it, in fascination, indifference, and grace; beneath it, in obscenity, weakness, and shame. He may be beyond anxiety in the former mode, but for once, in that whinny, we realize the price he pays for the austere control that is a life lived in gesture. Where critical interpretations of Chapter 31 mislead, then, is in their attempts to reduce Popeye to syphilis instead of seeing that he is more than the disease he inherits, including any symbolical or stereotyped connotations that the disease may suggest to

---

[16]Of course we see Popeye "whinny" in Temple's room earlier, in Chapter 18, but this is presented in the context of fascination: Temple's terror, the man's silent and eerie approach, the "whimper" of his "foreplay," and then, suddenly, the "high whinnying sound like a horse." This is not mediated by Minnie's reductive glance but by the detached report of the narrator. We are told nothing of the significance of Popeye's behavior, and while we may suspect impotence it is an impotence that is raised to incandescence!

us. He does not coincide with the past: he coexists with it, at a certain distance from it.

It is across the gesture that we find the *Faulknerian* dimension of Popeye, his place in a body of work that includes, for example, the Joe Christmas whose past had to be at once affirmed and denied. For is it not the case that in Faulkner's work the past is precisely that which is affirmed by the very actions that would deny it and that is denied by the very actions that affirm it? It is, of course, across such a play of affirmation and denial that we see such characters as Christmas, Sutpen, and Isaac McCaslin. But in Popeye we find the other side of the coin of character in Faulkner (as we may also see it in Flem Snopes). Where Sutpen, Christmas, and Ike McCaslin are articulators of the meaning of their lives, Popeye is silent about the significance of his own. It is we who must recognize the denial and affirmation that make up his life and that are at the heart of Faulkner's famous concern with "time." Chapter 31 exists in *Sanctuary* to remind us that we must do so. Sartre provides a language that makes it possible to speak that meaning and that helps us to avoid the dangers of what might be called the "reductionism of common sense" that have led some critics into understanding Popeye by reference to allegory and to psycho-somatic "just-so" stories.

In that Popeye who "stoically" (Brooks' word) accepts his death, we see the re-established Actor, that indifferent and transcendent "machine" inhabited by a ghost we cannot see but whose presence we experience through the "Others." Once again, on the scaffold, the Actor has an audience. It is the very bafflement of these bewildered onlookers (including critics) and their puzzlement as to his motives that allow us to see in Popeye more than an emblem of "modernity." The cigarette butts he uses to mark the day, his indifference to undeserved punishment, his bizarre request for "Ed Pinaud" hair lacquer—what are these if not a new set of gestures in a well-established structure? In the face of another threat to his autonomy (the kind of dismal end one might have predicted for an "underprivileged" child) such gestures secrete in Popeye a mysterious invulnerability to others. What is important is not "why" he allows himself to be killed for a crime he did not commit but that, once accused of such a crime, he behaves as one might expect of the Actor. He closes in on himself, wraps himself in the impenetrability of his indifference. Indifference to everything—at least on the stage of the world—is the law of Popeye's character. His last moments are in fundamental accord with the other moments of his public life. To use Sartre's well-known phrase to describe the self, Popeye is not what he is (delicate, weak, transparent to the gaze of the world) to the extent that he is what he is not (strong, brutal, opaque). His life, balanced in paradox, has as its pivot-point the gesture. Actor to the end, Popeye dies concerned only that his hair be in place.

Gothicism in *Sanctuary*:
The Black Pall and the Crap Table

by David L. Frazier

There are, I suggest, two large categories of elements in *Sanctuary*, the conventional Gothic and the unconventional modern; and the theme of society-directed indignation which characterizes the book is expressed, when it is not explicit, through satire effected by contrasting them. . . . In this connection the account of Red's wake, in chapter twenty-five, is a significant scene. In its relatively small wholeness may be more easily seen the general contrast . . ., the transition from the predominantly traditional condition with non-traditional touches to the predominantly non-traditional ending in which the contrasting traditionalism becomes vestigial, which forms the structure of the book as a whole. In it the Gothic and modern elements are mixed with compression, and from it are taken the terms used for convenience to denote these classes of elements—

> The archway to the dice room was draped in black. A black pall lay upon the crap table, upon which the overflow of floral shapes was beginning to accumulate. People entered steadily, the men in dark suits of decorous restraint, others in light, bright shades of spring, increasing the atmosphere of macabre paradox. (p. 292)

The scene sets a situation in which traditional behavior is demanded and in which there is at the start a predominantly suitable Gothic atmosphere, although incongruity exists in the crap table features and in the cast, whose attempts at fitting manners resemble apish mimicry. From the black pall and the crap table the action rushes along a catenation of contrasts with a bier and a bouncer, hymns and jazz, crosses and wreaths and bootleg booze, until their bestiality masters the actors and the wake becomes a funeral orgy in which even the semblance of traditional comportment vanishes and death and its trappings are stripped of their

"Gothicism in *Sanctuary*: The Black Pall and the Crap Table" by David L. Frazier. Extracted from *Modern Fiction Studies*, 2 (1956), 114–24. Copyright © by the Purdue Research Foundation, West Lafayette, Indiana 47907. Reprinted by permission of the publisher.

Gothic awfulness and dignity. In the beginning the crap table, at the end the black pall is incongruous; the passage is from a black pall to a crap table atmosphere, and the final effect is one of horrified disgust at the grotesque hoodlumism, at the backstage view of the Gothic scene, the wires, the grease paint, mummery disclosed. . . . The appropriateness of the scene, which is not a tightly integrated part of plot, is thematic; its theme is the breakdown of traditionalism implicit in the major action. It is the key to the largest function of Gothicism in the book.

. . . Faulkner's solution to the problem of maintaining suspense and pace—dramatic presentational form—is that with which early Gothicists met the problem; but his creation of the comic-terrible atmosphere is a significant departure from Gothic dramatic formula, significant because it parallels the transition in the story from the largely black pall to the largely crap table conditions. The action at the Old Frenchman place is close to Gothic conventionality; and, consistently, the mood is one of terror and the presentation formulistic. With the transition to Miss Reba's brothel, the modernistic locale, the element of comedy enters: the departure from formula coincides with the shift and corresponds with the breakdown of traditionalism in the plot movement. Comic interlude occurred in the Gothic romance on nothing like the scale in *Sanctuary*; a little comedy gave needed relief and by contrast intensified the horror, but it was strictly limited, from the danger of its marring the effect of high seriousness for which the early Gothicists strove. Comedy in *Sanctuary* begins small, with Miss Reba and her dogs, and has the intensifying effect, but soon grows large. Faulkner, approaching the close of the story, with the Clarence Snopes–train scene, the Virgil Snopes–bawdy house scene, the wake scene, the Uncle Bud–tea party scene brings horror and comedy to balance. . . .

Sanctuary begins, to repeat, in traditional form. The circumstances of the Old Frenchman place are largely conventional and establish the book's Gothicism. Perhaps the most conspicuous and highly conventionalized feature of Gothic formula was the setting; the locale of the action was almost invariably a massive dark building remote from civilization in the midst of wild nature, surrounded by a dark wood which deepened its gloom and air of foreboding. Setting is also a conspicuous feature of the first part of *Sanctuary* and conspicuously Gothic. From the first pages, with the reflecting pool, mysterious silence, descending darkness, deepening gloom, black jungle, and swooping owl Faulkner creates the atmosphere for a Gothic setting. Such elements make the proper frame for the Gothic building, and the Old Frenchman place looms from the blackness a proper Gothic ruin: "A moment later, above a black, jagged mass of trees, the house lifted its stark square bulk against the failing sky" (p. 6).

. . . But if it is largely a black pall ingredient . . . , its presentation is not completely traditional, for it is inhabited by no person of any sort whose presence is traditional. It is infested by a pack of vermin of a modern strain, bootleggers; and they, like the actors in the wake scene, are incongruous. The august ruined mansion calls for occupants of commensurate stature and of a nature consistent with its tone: if evil, grandly evil. But the bootleggers are at most animalistically vicious; in the mansion they seem creeping, crawling things; and this impression is enforced by the presence of the rats, with which in their movements, sounds, glowing eyes, and other traits the bootleggers are identifiable. The Gothic locale, too, has its crap table element; and the contrast feelingly implements the implicit moral judgment on bootlegging, bootleggers, and the society that produces them. . . .

The action at the Old Frenchman place is enough like a Gothic plot to prompt comparison, but in it the crap table strain becomes increasingly articulated. The plot of the old romance for which the Gothic structure was fabricated revolved about a crime, frequently one of illicit or incestuous love. This crime was the source of much of the horror in the tale, and the movement of the plot was toward prevention or retribution of it. So, too, the plot of *Sanctuary* revolves about a crime. The Gothic plot situation most like that of *Sanctuary*—the plot of Walpole's *The Castle of Otranto* exemplifies it—found a sterling maiden, separated from family and in a strange place (the Gothic locale), running about frenetically trying to escape being but ever on the verge of being deflowered by the monomaniacal villain; she was aided in her escape by the young hero and eventually saved by the appearance of her father. And this might serve as a sketch of the plot of *Sanctuary*, the skeleton of it, but it says nothing of the noteworthy variations which Faulkner makes upon tradition.

The centric sexual crime in *Sanctuary* is no conventional matter of illicit or incestuous love, though the story contains sufficiency of one and suggestion of the other; a crime involving either would have been too traditional, too human for Faulkner's purposes. Paradoxically, the conventional Gothic villain of the pursuing amorous sort is represented by Goodwin, who is not the villain. . . . Goodwin's pursuit creates the expectancy of conventional treatment, prepares the reader for a black pall crime; the crap table crime which actually occurs is therefore shocking. The contrast reveals in relief the pathology of Popeye's crime and effects augmented reprehension of modernism.

Similarly, the flight involved with the sexual crime is close to Gothic conventionality in broad outline, but has crap table qualifications which make it expressive of moral censure. Temple's situation bears obvious resemblance to that of the Gothic heroine; and she runs through the halls, rooms, stalls, trap doors, and lofts of the Old Frenchman place as the Gothic heroine ran through corridors, passageways innumerable in her flight from the villain. But thereafter the contrast enters: the Gothic heroine wanted only to escape, while Temple wants in part to be caught; and the flight of the heroine was wholly a flight of escape, while Temple's running is like an animalistic, feintingly evasive mating dance. Paradoxically, it is such that she lets herself be caught and such that it is actually a provocation. Implicit in the contrast is condemnation of the immorality of "modern" young womanhood, the flapperhood Temple personifies. It is an expression of the general attitude underlying the treatment of Little Belle, the girls on the train, the girls at Temple's university.

The object of the heroine's flight through the romance was a place of sanctuary. The corncrib in connection with Temple's flight is an important ironic element. Since it is so closely connected with the crimes that lie at the gravitational center of the book, and since it is the pivotal point in the plot's black pall to crap table turn and a symbolic focal point of the moral condemnation, the crib, with the word's connotation of the prostitute's workroom, is the most important of the several quasi-sanctuaries in the book. Temple, like the Gothic heroine, runs for sanctuary; but, unlike her, does not seek and find it in a holy place. Her refuge is the crib, and it suits her motivation; she both fled and sought her fate, and accordingly the crib figures as a place where she may escape her potential ravishment and a place where she may submit to it. . . . In the crib Temple prostitutes herself and is violated. The crib as temple is violated; the body as the temple is violated; Temple is violated. She is ravaged in turn, plowed . . . by a symbol of fecundity horribly used, through . . . one who represents evil in modern society, its tin gods mechanism, materialism, and perverted sexuality. The corncrib becomes a religious shrine appropriate to the unholy worship, and the prostitution-rape action a rite of the worship. With Temple, the movement of the plot with its increasing modernism comes to a climax in the corncrib, and there traditionalism dies. It is the pivotal point in the transition from the traditional with non-traditional touches to the non-traditional with Gothic overtones; after it Temple substitutes one kind of crib for another, and the movement which·began with the Gothic ruin and its elements of modernism proceeds to the modernistic locale of the brothel with its Gothic sights and sounds as a few remaining stimuli of traditional attitudes and values.

The parallel in *Sanctuary* to the key role of the father in the Gothic plot, a parallel, it may be, in which there are variations on the conventional Gothic element of prophecy about the crime and on the stock horror touch of the living statue and an expression of the recurrent idea of the blind inadequacy of legal justice as the agency of right, also comes to a crystallization in the crib. The prophecy may be indicated by Temple's cry, "I told you it was! .. I told you! It told you all the time!" (p. 122), the confirmation, perhaps, of a presentment she had tried to communicate to her father that because of the risks she ran in her escapades and her own vulnerability something like the rape would happen to her. The variation on the horror touch is the presentation of the blind man at the ruin as a living statue. When Temple first sees him she is terrified by his eyes, the blank eyes of a statue. He moves about the ruin with sculptured insentience. . . . His terror effect on Temple is constant, and the possibility that she prophesied to her father that something was going to happen to her may elucidate this effect. It may be that the statue represents her father, that his following her about corresponds to her father's constant presence in her thoughts at the Old Frenchman place, and that the statue's frightfulness is increased by fear she felt for her father, fear evoked because she is sexually tempted.

Judge Drake policed Temple's behavior and caused fear-based inhibitions in her, but gave her no sounder basis for ethical behavior; as a father he personified law. The relationship was inadequate for her needs; and she responded to the injunctions and the threats with resentment and took advantage of her opportunities to express by her actions her resentment and, indirectly, her need for understanding discipline and control. But her father was blind to what she was thereby trying to show him, and there is heavy irony in his being the judge, as Temple repeats over and over. It is to him, symbolized by the blind man, that she screams the I-told-you-so as the disaster approaches her with Popeye—

> She could hear silence in a thick rustling as he moved toward her through it, thrusting it aside, and she began to say Something is going to happen to me. She was saying it to the old man with the yellow clots for eyes. "Something is happening to me!" she screamed at him, sitting in his chair in the sunlight, his hands crossed on the top of the stick. "I told you it was!" she screamed . . . until he turned his head and the two phlegm clots above her where she lay tossing and thrashing on the rough, sunny boards. "I told you! I told you all the time!" (p. 122)

The interpretation may seem fanciful, but it explains a few otherwise obscure points in the book. Moreover, the image of Judge Drake presented at the end of the book calls up irresistibly the image of the blind man: "Beside her, her father sat, his hands crossed on the head of his stick . . ." (p. 379). If it is correct, it represents an interesting adaptation of the conventional Gothic usage of the father.

The heroine of the romance found herself in her plight because her father was not present to protect her. That Temple's father is absent during her nightmare in the ruin, then, is conventional. But there is a more important sense in which his absence results in her predicament, and that is in his absence as a proper father from the first. Not physical presence, but guidance to assure safety in parental absence is necessary for the emancipated heroine which Temple is. But Judge Drake is inadequate, and he shares with society the blame for Temple's catastrophe. His failure to save the heroine as the Gothic father saved her is the consequence that illuminates his general moral failure. The Gothic father's arrival is parodied, because Temple's father arrives too late; the catastrophe has befallen her, and she is totally corrupted. He remains blind and inadequate to the last: her predicament is moral, but he removes her only from its physical setting, the whore house, and attempts to set things right by giving her a trip to Europe. The presentation is a modern twist given conventionality, and he emerges a part of reprehensible modernism.

Religion, not only the sort of which Popeye is the priest or icon, but also traditionalistic religion enters largely into *Sanctuary* as it did in the romance, where it was usually a force working for the right and occasionally a horror device employed for its mystery value. But in *Sanctuary* religion is neither good nor black in an occult sense; it is devoid of any supernaturalistic connection. It is no source of consolation or of sanctuary; it is blind, dogmatic unreason, prejudice with fanatic zeal; the right for which it works is morally wrong, and its working hampers justice and fosters inequities. The minister's sermon which Benbow recounts to Miss Jenny may well have been the germ of the idea that, given impetus by the district attorney, led the mob to drag Goodwin from jail and burn him alive. It was a committee of religious ladies that hounded Ruby and her sick child from the hotel where Benbow placed them. When the time of judgment came in the Gothic plot, poetic justice of divine rightness, often tempered with mercy, was meted out. Justice in *Sanctuary* is vicious and blind and fits neither the crimes nor the virtues of the characters. It is not divine, but legal justice; and the blindness and inadequacy of law is the last ironic twist of the knife. Religion fails to promote justice, and without religion law cannot succeed.

Horace Benbow represents the union of morality and law and is the foil of Judge Drake. He tries to save Little Belle as Judge Drake did not try to save Temple; he works for the right judgment upon Goodwin which the law confounds and Judge Drake thwarts. Benbow exerts the only motive force toward the right which is operative in *Sanctuary*; but it is, of course, direction frustrated: the opposed collective maleficent force of modernism is finally overwhelming. Much could be said of Benbow and of Ruby Lamar, the other major approvable character in the book, but their Gothic qualities need no great elaboration. It is perhaps sufficient to say of Benbow in this connection that he personifies the traditional values of the Gothic romance in the modern conditions of *Sanctuary* and that his failure is the failure of traditionalism. Ruby bears

strong resemblance to the suffering matron figure in the romance . . . .
Loyalty and fidelity, too, are the keynotes of Ruby's character; but they
are of a kind that transcends narrow moral definition. She is a whore of
necessity, but she is uncorrupted; she is the foil, then, of Temple, who is
not a whore but is spiritually rotten. Ruby is not, either, religious in the
conventional way of the Gothic matron, but has her own naturalistic
ethic in which love, hard work, and honesty are the main principles.
Ruby is the virtuous Gothic matron as she can only exist in modern
society; and the differences between Ruby and the matron are the effects
of, and point up, the evils of modern society. She embodies the basic
virtues which neither perverted sexuality, parental failure, vicious law,
nor corrupted religion can destroy.

Ruby, as teller of truth, describes exactly what Temple is with the one
word *honest*, employing all the traditional ironic values of the word: "Oh,
I know your sort. . . . Honest women" (p. 66). The irony of Temple
Drake is that while she is placed in the role of the Gothic heroine and
resembles her superficially in several respects—enough to establish the
identification so that her unlike qualities are the more striking—she is,
beneath all, worse than whore because a selfish hypocrite who gives
nothing for all she receives. The sentimental heroine was customarily
chaste, knew no evil. Temple was a virgin before the crib, but only
technically; she had no virginal attitudes and therefore no purity of mind
as armor against evil as had the Gothic damsel. The evil which overcame
Temple came in part from within her. She was not raped, but seduced—
perhaps merely given opportunity. Removed from her father and
brothers, her inhibitors, her concupiscence, a result of the corrupting
influence of modern society, begins to control her; and she submits to
her latent nature as frenziedly as she ran from and toward it before. In
the middle portion of the action, after the pivotal rape scene, she
undergoes the typical black pall to crap table changes. She changes from
the Gothic heroine with unconventional qualities to a creature of modernism, a nymphomaniac, with Gothic overtones—

> When he [Red] touched her she sprang like a bow, hurling herself
> upon him, her mouth gaped and ugly . . . as she writhed her loins
> against him.
> . . . With her hips grinding against him, her mouth gaping in
> straining protrusion, bloodless, she began to speak. "Let's hurry.
> Anywhere." (p. 287)

The image of Temple in the entire scene is striking in its ugliness, and the
effect owes much to the blending of black pall and crap table motifs, the
blending of the vampire and the vamp.

In the closing action Temple again becomes identifiable with the
Gothic heroine; and the change from the first of the book to the last

parallels Benbow's vision in the episode involving the photograph of Little Belle (p. 200). The photograph, one of the most effective variations on the magical glass imagery which includes the pool at the beginning, the mirror in which Benbow detects Little Belle's dissimulation, the clock in the brothel, and the compact used by Temple in the end, discloses the eternal expression in pure form of the propensity to evil which characterizes Little Belle, Temple, and all women back to Eve. The image, with the precarious balancing, the shifting, the distorted but clear vision of evil, the flattening, and the vacant musing, suggests a schematization of the changes Temple undergoes in the course of the novel.

What Temple is to the heroine, Gowan Stevens is to the Gothic hero; and he is an even more obvious parody on Gothic convention. Among the peasants of Mississippi he by virtue of his Virginia education and alcohol is a notable youth, a gentleman. So Benbow describes him: " 'The Virginia gentleman one, who told us . . . about how they taught him to drink like a gentleman. Put a beetle in alcohol, and you have a scarab; put a Mississippian in alcohol, and you have a gentleman' " (p. 29). Faulkner draws him with heavy sarcasm. The Gothic hero too, like Theodore in *Otranto*, was often a noble youth among peasants in some disguise. Further, the hero had flawless virtue, a heart of gold, and absolute courage; and after his accidental involvement with the heroine he did all in his power, faced death bravely, to save her. Stevens' courage is drunken bellicosity, his honor a parody on the medieval conception. Instead of finding the heroine in her plight, Stevens puts her into it. He realizes that he is obligated to protect her—" 'Got proteck . . .' Gowan muttered '. . . girl. 'Ginia gem . . . gemman got proteck . . .' " (p. 86). And he picks a fight with Van, gets beaten up, and passes the night in a drunken stupor. When Temple needs him most he fails her, leaves her in her plight because of his shame at not having held his liquor like a gentleman. In his farewell letter to Narcissa he discloses that he, like Theodore, is afflicted with a great soul-sadness; it is a burlesque upon even Sentimental self-pity. Stevens is the jellybean in Faulkner's general moral condemnation of modern youth.

As might be expected, Popeye is a prime exemplification of the black pall and crap table relationship in the book. He begins as the monster and ends as the criminal; he is the personification of evil, the equivalent of the Gothic villain, and the gangster, a case for sociological study. In his final effect he is the personification of evil still; but of social evil, and a monster, but a Frankenstinian monster whose creator was society. He is a human, but in his mechanism and amorality hardly recognizable as human. He is a demon, but neither his origins nor powers are supernatural; and accordingly his demonical attributes are all normally modern: his glowing eye is a cigarette, the smoke that accompanies him tobacco smoke, his demoniacal aura the smell of brilliantine, his deathly power a deadly pistol. . . .

It is unimportant that Popeye, like the usual Gothic villain, is an Italian; it does, however, matter that he has a physical defect, as the Gothic villain often had. Popeye is impotent, and since he represents death forces alone this is a symbolic defect. The pistol, the machine consistent with his mechanism, is a more appropriate phallic symbol in *Sanctuary* than it usually is in literature where it functions as such. It ejaculates death; and the irony of Popeye's circumstance is that since he wishes to possess Temple he cannot use upon her even his phallic substitute, but must bring in Red and the danger of losing her. Popeye's dilemma arises from the fact that he is not totally inhuman; for so long as he is mastered by no desire—and Popeye is an ironically ascetic figure— he is invincible. His desire for Temple, then, is an ironic twist upon the tragic flaw of the conventional amorous Gothic villain, who was good except for the evil sexual obsession that brought about his downfall. Paradoxically, sexual desire, in Popeye's case, brings about the downfall of evil; it is a life force that defeats death. Popeye's is an internal collapse; he does not wish to escape death. And perhaps it is his dilemma, his awareness of his own black futility, that keeps him deathly impassive until he is mechanically flipped off, dropped by society to dangle like its puppet.

To a large degree the horror and mystery, and therefore the very Gothicism, of the Gothic romance was a cumulative effect of the battery of stock props and devices included in it. Certain uses of these elements in *Sanctuary*, the dark woods, the ruin, the owl, the statue, the objects of the magical glass sort, and others, have been mentioned. To them could be added the corpses, the blood, the mysterious sounds, the tomb imagery in Temple's hallucination, the incubus-quality of her night in the room at the ruin, the suggestion of the Cannibal Bridegroom motif in her wild rides with Popeye. These, along with conventionalities of pre- sentational mode, plot, character types, give *Sanctuary* a markedly Gothicesque quality. Yet, however Gothicesque it may be, *Sanctuary* is more than the old romance and different. It is not simply a tale of terror, not simply, as Faulkner called it, the "most horrific tale" (p. vi) that he could contrive. The Gothic elements contribute to the horror . . . of the book, but their . . . effectiveness has become lessened, staled, in time; and therefore their main effect is to highlight the greater horribleness of the modern elements with which they are linked.

In addition, and more importantly, the Gothic elements are evocative of traditional values which serve as implicit standards by which the modern conditions may be judged. In a sense, then, the elements serve as stimuli of stock responses; they create pendent expectancy of conventional treatments and suggest that traditional values the conventional treatments embody. When the presentation of a character, an action, a setting suggests identification with Gothic convention, that convention becomes a standard with which the presentation is implicitly compared. Should the presentation deviate from conventional expectation, the deviation is therefore distinctly noticeable. If the deviation conflicts with the moral values inherent in, associated with, the convention, it is seen as moral deviation. And in so far as this deviation is identifiable with modern conditions, modern behavior, modernism is implicitly condemned. With modification suitable to particular instances of its application, then, this is the mode of expression of outrage employed throughout the book. If the Gothic qualities or the deviations are sensational, still *Sanctuary* is not spectacular in the way of the old romance, in which the spectacle was its own end. The sensationalism *Sanctuary* contains is necessary for the force of its criticism; because of the contrast process no element, black pall or crap table, however shocking, is merely sensational in its final effect.

William Faulkner's "Temple" of Innocence

by Aubrey Williams

Critical opinion about *Sanctuary* has ranged from the views of those who have read it in psychological terms as an expression of man's fear of sexual impotence to the views of those who have read it in more or less sociological terms as an attack on exploitive modernism. The latter view has been most widely held, and essential to it is the idea that the gangster Popeye is a symbol, or allegorical figure, of all that is most inhuman in modern capitalistic society. . . .

There is, however, much in *Sanctuary* to upset a straightforward equation of Popeye with "modernism," and to suggest instead that he is ultimately representative of an evil more primal and profound than that which one might identify with some particular political or economic system. . . . But Popeye is best defined by the context afforded him by the novel as a whole.

I

The most significant, and the most disregarded, aspect of *Sanctuary* is the novel's preoccupation with children and childishness, and with the inevitable participation of these children in evil. This theme of the inevitable participation of the young in the world of adult evil underlies and informs two of the novel's most comic episodes: the sojourn of the two Snopes boys in Miss Reba's whore-house (which they take to be a boarding-house), and the same madam's genteel beer party. Certainly the broad outline of the episode in which the Snopes boys discover, only gradually and after some weeks of residence, the real nature of their "hotel" suggests the transition from a kind of "innocence" to knowledge. This same theme is apparent in the episode following Red's funeral, when Miss Reba and her fellow madams entertain themselves

"William Faulkner's 'Temple' of Innocence" by Aubrey Williams. Extracted from the *Rice Institute Pamphlet*, 47, No. 3 (Oct. 1960), 51–67. Reprinted by permission of the author and the publisher.

with polite conversation over beer and gin. Uncle Bud, the bullet-headed little boy of five or six, has struck at one of Miss Reba's dogs:

> The dog's head snapped around, its teeth clicking, its half-hidden eyes bright and malevolent. The boy recoiled. "You bite me, you thon bitch," he said.
>
> "Uncle Bud!" the fat woman said, her round face, rigid in fatty folds and streaked with tears, turned upon the boy in shocked surprise, the plumes nodding precariously above it. . . . "The very idea!" the fat woman said. "How in the world he can learn such words on an Arkansaw farm, I don't know."
>
> "They'll learn meanness anywhere," Miss Reba said.

A moment later one of the ladies asks about Miss Reba's two boarders, the Snopes boys:

> "Is them two nice young fellows still with you, Miss Reba?"
>
> "Yes," Miss Reba said. "I think I got to get shut of them, though. I aint specially tender-hearted, but after all it aint no use in helping young folks to learn this world's meanness until they have to. I already had to stop the girls running around the house without no clothes on, and they don't like it."

The "world's meanness," of course, is only Miss Reba's crude vision of the world of human evil. Elsewhere in the novel the idea of the young becoming aware of human evil and of their own participation in it is placed in more traditional contexts, as in the following meditation of Temple while in the Memphis brothel:

> She was thinking about half-past-ten-oclock. The hour for dressing for a dance, if you were popular enough not to have to be on time. The air would be steamy with recent baths, and perhaps powder in the light like chaff in barn-lofts, and they looking at one another, comparing, talking whether you could do more damage if you could just walk out on the floor like you were now. Some wouldn't, mostly ones with short legs. Some of them were all right, but they just wouldn't. They wouldn't say why. The worst one of all said boys thought all girls were ugly except when they were dressed. She said the Snake had been seeing Eve for several days and never noticed her until Adam made her put on a fig leaf. How do you know? they said, and she said because the Snake was there before Adam, because he was the first one thrown out of heaven: he was there all the time. But that wasn't what they meant and they said, How do you know? and Temple thought of her kind of backed up against the dressing table and the rest of them in a circle around her with their combed hair and their shoulders smelling of scented

soap and the light powder in the air and their eyes like knives until you could almost watch her flesh where the eyes were touching it, and her eyes in her ugly face courageous and frightened and daring, and they all saying, How do you know? until she told them and held up her hand and swore she had. That was when the youngest one turned and ran out of the room. She locked herself in the bath and they could hear her being sick.

The teen-age theodicy of this passage is not, presumably, Faulkner's own, yet the view of the world, the flesh and the devil it expresses relates directly to a view of the world explored and probed by the novel as a whole. For without making any great claim for theological nicety on Faulkner's part, it is yet essential to understand that much of the shocking impact of *Sanctuary* derives ultimately from the fact that Faulkner is working from, and within, a certain Southern metaphysic which has, in some of its more rigorous and puritanical aspects, at least a tendency towards a kind of Manichaeism, a tendency to equate sex with evil and to view nature as totally depraved. The harsh and stark assumptions which Faulkner has chosen to explore in the novel are, for all practical purposes, closely akin to those of Calvin, especially as they might be suggested by such a passage from Calvin as this:

And therefore infants themselves, as they bring their condemnation into the world with them, are rendered obnoxious to punishment by their own sinfulness, not by the sinfulness of another. For though they have not yet produced the fruits of their iniquity, yet they have the seed of it within them; even their whole nature is as it were a seed of sin, and therefore cannot be odious and abominable to God. . . . For our nature is not only destitute of all good, but is so fertile in all evils that it cannot remain inactive . . . every thing in man, the understanding and will, the soul and body, is polluted and engrossed by . . . concupiscence.

This is not to imply, of course, that Faulkner read Calvin and then wrote *Sanctuary*. Faulkner may never have read the *Institutes* at all, and Calvin is only cited here as a convenient background against which we may view the theme of the novel as a whole, and also against which we may view one of the dominant symbols of the novel—Ruby Lamar's baby. This infant appears in scene after scene throughout *Sanctuary*, silently expressing by its blighted and ubiquitous presence the agony to which it and all the other "children" of the book have been born. The baby was born out of wedlock, a point made perhaps to suggest that it was "born in sin," fathered by Lee Goodwin. Twice it is described as lying as if it were crucified. On other occasions it lies with "its hands upflung beside its head, as though it had died in the presence of an

agony which had not had time to touch it." Born in sin, Faulkner seems
to say, the child is already blighted by the evil inherent in human nature,
an evil of which the child is not yet aware, but an evil which it will
inevitably "learn" and perpetuate.

The growth and fructification of the "seed of sin" within all children
is, then, the major area of human experience explored by the novel.
Moreover, an awareness or recognition of this maturation process, in
one's self or in others, is seen as a kind of death, an emphasis of the novel
which vividly recalls the passage in Genesis where God says that Adam
and Eve will surely die if they eat of the tree of knowledge of good and
evil. Horace Benbow expresses this idea clearly when he says that

> perhaps it is upon the instant that we realize, admit, that there is a
> logical pattern to evil, that we die, he thought, thinking of the
> expression he had once seen in the eyes of a dead child, and of
> other dead: the cooling indignation, the shocked despair fading,
> leaving two empty globes in which the motionless world lurked
> profoundly in miniature.

It is this idea too which gives symbolic significance to the death of
Tommy just before Temple's shocking experience of evil at the hands of
Popeye, the rape which deprives her of any "innocence" she may be
thought to have had and forcibly introduces her to the depravity for
which she had an affinity from the start. Tommy is a thirty-year-old
child. Feeble-minded, he cannot "grow up" to adult awareness of evil,
cannot mature in evil. After his death the townspeople remember him
only as "barefoot, hatless, with his rapt, empty gaze and his cheek bulged
innocently by a peppermint jaw-breaker." But, killed by Popeye the
instant before Temple's rape, Tommy's death serves to suggest, in
somewhat ritualistic fashion, the "death" of Temple's "childhood" and
her introduction to adult and evil "reality." That she has only entered
into a kind of death is also plainly indicated by the conclusion of the
novel. Listening to a concert in the Luxembourg Gardens, she "seemed
to follow with her eyes the waves of music, to dissolve into the dying
brasses, across the pool and the opposite semi-circle of trees where at
sombre intervals the dead tranquil queens in stained marble mused, and
on into the sky lying prone and vanquished in the embrace of the season
of rain and death."

It is in terms of Temple herself that the image and idea of childishness
has its most obvious development. Throughout her stay in the decayed
Frenchman's Bend mansion her appearance and manner repeatedly
evoke the traditional images of childhood. She peers "around the door
with the wide, abashed curiosity of a child." She has been "playing at it
[sex]," she is told by Ruby, the woman who has seen her lover shot down
at her feet by her own father and who has prostituted herself for

Goodwin. Temple is told she is not "meeting kids" now, but still she looks like an "elongated and leggy infant in her scant dress and uptilted hat." Later she sits on the cot at Frenchman's Bend, looking quite "small, her very attitude an outrage to muscle and tissue of more than seventeen and more compatible with eight or ten." She is "long-legged, thin armed, with high small buttocks—a small childish figure no longer quite a child, nor yet quite a woman." On the way to Memphis with Popeye she opens "her mouth in that round, hopeless expression of a child." In Miss Reba's establishment, "Lying on her back, her legs close together, she began to cry, hopelessly and passively, like a child in a dentist's waiting-room." Such examples as these by no means exhaust the images and associations of childhood with which Faulkner invests Temple, nor do they suggest the many similar images which characterize most of the incidental figures in the novel: the crowds of college students Horace Benbow encounters on the train, with their puppyish squeals and pawings; Gowan Stevens, one of the "little shirt-tale boys" who "are too young to realize that people don't break the law just for a holiday." What happens to these children is analogous to what happens to Miss Reba's two woolly, shapeless dogs: "savage, petulant, spoiled, the flatulent monotony of their sheltered lives snatched up without warning by an incomprehensible moment of terror and fear of bodily annihilation at the very hands which symbolized by ordinary the licensed tranquillity of their lives."

II

Temple's experience is the exemplification, pushed to a terrible extreme, of the novel's assumption that the maturing process is inevitably a process of learning about one's own involvement in evil. The experience may come violently, shockingly, as with Temple; it may come less violently, though hardly less vulgarly, as with Benbow's step-daughter, Little Belle.

It is in the person of Horace Benbow, however, that the meaning of *Sanctuary* is best perceived. The novel is far more his story than it is Temple's, for it is in and through his development and perceptions that we ourselves arrive at an understanding of the book's meaning. Usually Benbow is dismissed as the ineffectual idealist, but this is too much of an oversimplification. He is the most fully rounded of the novel's characters, and he undergoes a development that is analogous to that of Temple and all the other "children" in the book. He too becomes acquainted with the night.

Benbow is, as critics have noted, an idealist, and his development in the novel is toward an awareness of the "reality" postulated by the book.

We should note carefully, however, the metaphorical terms of his ideal-
ism. During the course of Goodwin's imprisonment, for example,
Benbow is unable to comprehend Goodwin's fear of Popeye. Goodwin,
on the other hand, thinks Benbow's trust in human justice to be naïve
and childish. At one point he says to Benbow: "What sort of men have
you lived with all your life? In a nursery?"

In a sense Benbow has lived the protected life of a nursery. He has
always been surrounded and subjugated by women; he is, quite truly, a
forty-three-year-old child who has suddenly been confronted with the
awful fact of human evil. He is first shocked into awareness by his step-
daughter, Little Belle. The extent of his shocked revulsion is made clear
at the very beginning of the novel, for it opens with Benbow running,
very much like a small boy, away from home. What started him running,
he says, was a "rag with rouge on it." He found the rag stuffed behind the
mirror in Little Belle's room, and to him it is evidently the sign of his
step-daughter's first sexual experience. The fact that Little Belle likes to
pick up strange young men on trains and to pet with them in the grape
arbor also disturbs Benbow, and he soon begins to have a vision in which
the overlay of sweetness and innocence on Little Belle's face is replaced
by the incipient evil lurking just beneath the surface. As he gazes upon
Little Belle's photograph,

> the image blurred into the high-light, like something familiar seen
> beneath disturbed though clear water; he looked at the familiar
> image with a kind of quiet horror and despair, at a face suddenly
> older in sin than he would ever be, a face more blurred than sweet,
> at eyes more secret than soft.

Later on, after Benbow has been to Memphis and heard Temple's
account of her rape, he returns home and again gazes on the photograph. This time the life of his step-daughter fuses into the experience
undergone by Temple:

> the face appeared to breathe in his palms in a shallow bath of
> highlight, beneath the slow, smokelike tongues of invisible honey-
> suckle. Almost palpable enough to be seen, the scent filled the
> room and the small face seemed to swoon in a voluptuous languor,
> blurring still more, fading, leaving upon his eye a soft and fading
> aftermath of invitation and voluptuous promise and secret affirma-
> tion like a scent itself.
>
>   Then he knew what that sensation in his stomach meant. He put
> the photograph down hurriedly and went to the bathroom. He
> opened the door running and fumbled at the light. But he had not
> time to find it and he gave over and plunged forward and struck the
> lavatory and leaned upon his braced arms while the shucks set up a

terrific uproar beneath her thighs. Lying with her head lifted slightly, her chin depressed like a figure lifted down from a crucifix, she watched something black and furious go roaring out of her pale body.

Since it is Benbow himself who equates Popeye's smell with "that black stuff that ran out of Bovary's mouth," it does not seem too ingenious to extend the reference to the "something black and furious" which goes roaring out of Little Belle's (or Temple's) pale body, or to the vomiting of the young girl in the dormitory when she is made aware for the first time of the sexual experience of her girl friend, or even ultimately to the vomiting of the little boy, Uncle Bud, when he gets drunk on beer at Miss Reba's, to Gowan Stevens' vomiting when he comes to his own miserable little awareness, and to Benbow's vomiting in the passage just cited. All these instances illustrate, with varying degrees of comedy and pathos, the shock resulting from first experience with adult evil. Safeguarded as he has been by the cloak of maternal solicitude and by his idealistic beliefs in the traditional code of the gentleman, Benbow's experience of "sex" and "evil" and "reality," as these are defined and for all practical purposes *equated* in the novel, has been much delayed.

Benbow is a lawyer who believes that justice will always triumph and that God is a Gentleman Who will see that a certain decency is maintained in human affairs. Opposed to his view, of course, is the whole weight of the novel's action, but perhaps his point of view is best contrasted with that of his Aunt Jenny, a realist who manages to view life clearly and to be compassionate and decent at the same time. When Benbow states that he cannot "stand idly by and see injustice," Aunt Jenny remarks: "You won't ever catch up with injustice, Horace." Appalled by what Temple experiences as a result of Gowan Stevens' folly, Benbow cannot reconcile himself to the fact that a woman may be exposed to the most monstrous forms of evil through mere human foolishness. To this Aunt Jenny responds by asking him if he intends to "start some kind of roach campaign?" Benbow thinks that evil can be legislated out, stamped out, of existence. He would like to have a law passed which would make it obligatory "upon everyone to shoot any man less than fifty years old that makes, buys, sells or thinks whiskey." Then, he thinks, such things as Temple's rape would not occur. He thinks it reassuring to say to Goodwin: "You've got the law, justice, civilization" on your side. He believes that evil can be cleansed from human nature, that it can be "removed, cauterized out of the old and tragic flank of the world."

We should note that Benbow, no matter how pure and idealistic his motives, is constantly under the suspicion of all the other members of the community, including Aunt Jenny. Benbow is suspected by Clarence

Snopes of going to the Memphis brothel not merely to find Temple, but also for purposes of debauchery. Ruby Lamar thinks he wishes to be paid for his legal services by sleeping with her, and this is also the view of Aunt Jenny and everyone else. And the community's assumptions, indeed, are the assumptions so starkly explored and revealed, and to a great extent confirmed, by the action of the novel. This unflagging suspicion of motives which characterizes the community's view of human nature is not simply an affinity for evil; in a world such as that depicted in *Sanctuary* it is rather, as Faulkner himself says at one point, the course of "practical wisdom."

Benbow's trust in the law and in justice invites, of course, the most painful disillusionment. The evil defined by the actions and events in *Sanctuary* is seen to be too much of the essence of human nature for any legal cauterization. To drive this point home Faulkner presents us with two trials, those of Goodwin and Popeye, which are such savagely ironic miscarriages of justice. In each trial a man is convicted and then executed for a crime he did not commit. Faulkner goes to the extreme of coincidence in his anxiety for the reader to notice the common element in the two trials. In each case the defendant's lawyer is ineffectual, the two juries are out exactly eight minutes each, and the verdicts are the same. The same ineffectual nature of human, as well as divine, justice is conveyed earlier when Temple tries to stave off the horror of her situation at Frenchman's Bend by saying to herself again and again, "My father's a judge. My father's a judge."

Benbow emerges from the courtroom in which Goodwin is wrongfully condemned, because of Temple's perjury, "like an old man, with a drawn face." Crushed by his new awareness, he returns to the home and woman from whom he had fled. He has learned, presumably, that one cannot "run away" from evil, and he is also to be seen as overwhelmed by the knowledge that his own good intentions have contributed, directly or indirectly, to Goodwin's violent death in a bonfire.

III

If the above account of the novel's main issues and themes is in any way correct, then it would appear that Popeye is representative of something other than a kind of "modernism." For one thing, there is the comparison of Popeye to the black stuff that pours out of Emma Bovary's mouth, a blackness which is certainly to be equated with evil and corruption. This symbol in turn relates Popeye to all the other vomiting which takes place in Faulkner's characters when they first participate in adult evil. Popeye is called "the little black man," he wears black suits, he has eyes like black rubber knobs. Popeye is the blackness, the vomit, the evil.

Just as important, however, is the fact that Popeye is repeatedly described as having the body of a child. He twists and pinches "cigarettes in his little, doll-like hands." He lurks around corners, "smoking his cigarettes, like a sullen and sick child." To Temple, Popeye's arm "felt frail, no larger than a child's." In his childhood a doctor had said of him: "he will never be a man, properly speaking. With care he will live sometime longer. But he will never be any older than he is now."

The effect which Faulkner achieves by placing full-blown and cold adult depravity in the body of a child is very similar to the effect Swift achieves in placing perfect rationality in the bodies of his horses, the Houyhnhmns. A monster is the result in both instances, but in *Sanctuary* it is a monster which places in transparent clarity the main assumption that Faulkner has chosen to explore: the assumption, that is, that in each child there is a seed of sin or evil which will in time ripen into full iniquity. The evil which exists in the other children of the novel as a kind of potency, is seen to exist in the childish body of Popeye in full actuality. This juxtaposition of his childlike body with his full-blown adult depravity is a distortion, but one by which the mind is given, in a moment of startling superimposure, a vision of the seed and of the fruit into which it will ripen (much as the "crib" in which Temple is raped suggests not only the cradle but also the stall of the prostitute). It is perhaps the grimmest representation in all literature of the idea that the child is father to the man.

The grotesque duality of Popeye's nature is such that he exists primarily on the level of symbolic significance; he has the "depthless quality of stamped tin," as Faulkner says. And it is in terms of this grotesque duality of his nature that we are to account for the fact that he cannot spend satisfactorily the money he makes, cannot drink the whiskey he bootlegs, cannot enjoy the woman he "rapes." He has all the motives, desires and instincts of adult evil, but his childlike body provides him with none of the means of satisfying his desires.

The monstrous quality of Popeye's existence makes him appear not only inhuman but also inscrutable, and thus he reflects the face which evil always offers to the human understanding. This inscrutability is dramatized in the closing episode of his life, when he is shown to be inhumanly indifferent to his own death. We may see in Popeye an embodiment of the evil within men, but he must finally be left as essentially mysterious. All the good artist has ever been able to do is to give us a name for evil, and thereby perhaps make its darkness visible.

IV

The world of *Sanctuary* is a world in which God, if He is to be conceived as existing at all, has been reduced to an equation with man himself, identified with, and comprehended solely in terms of, human existence. Thus when Benbow says of God that "at least He's a gentleman," Ruby Lamar replies, "I always thought of Him as a man." The theme of the crucifixion permeates *Sanctuary*, but it is man himself, whether it be Ruby Lamar's baby or Temple Drake or Lee Goodwin, who is presented as the crucified. Operating as it does within the framework of the Christian myth, the novel yet understands the myth solely in human terms. Instead of Christian theology, Faulkner gives us a kind of Christian humanology.

The world of *Sanctuary* is the world envisioned by Temple as she lies in the Memphis whore-house. She watches the face of a clock in the semi-darkness, and soon the round orifice of the clock seems to change to a "disc suspended in nothingness, the original chaos, and change in turn to a crystal ball holding in its still and cryptic depths the ordered chaos of the intricate and shadowy world upon whose scarred flanks the old wounds whirl onward at dizzy speed into darkness lurking with new disasters." Again and again we are given this image of a world marooned in space, a dying planet revolving to the moment when it will be a dead mass suspended in nothingness.

The inhabitants of this dying planet are continually exhibited as the victims and prisoners of the very pattern of evil which they themselves help to create and perpetuate, though it is also a pattern which they never really understand. Faulkner imparts the sense of this by two overlapping patterns of imagery, one of which repeatedly describes the way in which men and women are seized by the scruff of the neck, like kittens or puppies, and then hurled into disaster by those who in their turn are also ultimately seized by the neck. The other pattern of imagery also focuses on man's neck, and again man's neck is repeatedly seen as stretched or prepared, or shaven for the noose, the knife, or the guillotine. Thus when Benbow boards a train he finds the day-coach filled "with bodies sprawled half into the aisle as though in the aftermath of a sudden and violent destruction, with dropped heads, open-mouthed, their throats turned profoundly upward as though waiting the stroke of knives."

Of the agony and terror suffered by the inhabitants of this world there can be no doubt. Almost all the characters are eventually presented in terms which recall the pathetic and hopeless grieving of little children in the face of incomprehensible suffering, even though these same children are destined to grow up and in their turn cause the most intense agony to themselves and to others. All of them have difficulty in breathing the air of this world into which they have come: even Gowan Stevens, snoring helplessly and painfully through his shattered nose; even Miss Reba, gasping in horrid and painful asthmatic breaths her grief for Mr. Binford; even Ruby's baby, who breathes in "weak, whistling gasps."

The world of *Sanctuary* offers little or nothing in the way of protection from suffering or in the way of solace for loss. It is a world of darkness in which the only gleam of light is that cast by intermittent fireflies, in which the only sound to come to man is that of some nameless wood-bird—three bars, perhaps, "in monotonous repetition: a sound meaningless and profound out of a suspirant and peaceful following silence" which seems to strand man in uttermost darkness. It is a world in which the very air is spent and defunctive, in which all life dies and all death lives, a world that is flatulent, stale and moribund.

That Faulkner regards the inhabitants of this world with a kind of savage pity seems undeniable. Stark and strange and stern as his vision of man is, he yet presents man as the victim not only of himself, but also as the victim of a world, and pattern of evil, for which he is not fully responsible: man is not only the crucifier, but the crucified. To say this is not, of course, to minimize the shocking horror of the world one finds in *Sanctuary*; it is rather to underscore and emphasize the horror. The true and ultimate shock of the novel is not to be found in the single grotesque episode in which a young girl is raped with a corn-cob. It is to be found in the larger pattern of evil and injustice of which this episode is one mere instance. It is a pattern of evil and a vision of the world which is hardly comparable with any thing else Faulkner has written, though it does have important unexplored connections with the rest of his work. In this novel at least, Faulkner presents us with the bleak assertion that the human body is not a temple of the holy spirit, and with the equally bleak assertion that, for man, there is no sanctuary.

The Pattern of Nightmare in *Sanctuary*; or, Miss Reba's Dogs

by William Rossky

Much of the feeling of *Sanctuary* is the result of what we may well call a technique of nightmare. Although the word "nightmare" is hardly an original one for the novel, how thoroughly it applies requires emphasis. Repeatedly the narrative evokes moments of dreamlike horror typical especially of a certain kind of nightmare: The dreamer is caught in impotent terror; paralyzed, deeply frightened, trying, yet unable, to act or to scream. And while they provide an appropriate atmosphere for the patterns of degenerate modernity, these many instances of paralysis-with-horror also contribute even more to a sense of cosmic nightmare; they accumulate to an experience of profound terror and powerlessness within and before the chaos and illogicality of the whole of existence.

This view is clarified and supported by the recurrent examples of nightmare imagery. And I do not refer here merely to what might be called modern variations on the conventions of the older Gothic novel—such matters as the moldering old ruin, the Frenchman's place, which duplicates the decaying medieval castle; the threat of a dark villain in Popeye's lean, lethal shadow extending over the house; or the figure of the half frightening and half protective retainer. Although such things contribute to the total tone, the chills inspired by these and similar conventional Gothic devices arise clearly out of make-believe. Almost like the shudders of children listening to tales of haunted houses, they are the fears of "let's pretend." The effects are not deeply disturbing, not genuinely nightmarish, and Faulkner leaves them behind rather early in the book. More deeply woven into its texture, however, are the dreamlike images and scenes in which the principals—and the readers—are caught in a clotting motion, in a paralysis, or near-paralysis, of helpless terror. . . .

These moments of fear-infused stasis that convey the sense of impotence of nightmare begin on the first pages with that still and threatening two-hour pause, broken only by an occasional bird call or the sound from the highway, during which Horace squats before the danger of Popeye at the spring. They appear repeatedly in the experience of Temple Drake and, incidentally, help to create a degree of identification with her that is sometimes overlooked. Especially at the Frenchman's place, Temple seems almost constantly in motion that yet remains terrifyingly fixed; she seems constantly wheeling to flee from one room to another and back again, yet remains in one place, in the circle of the house, cowering in the circle of her fear: "Still running her bones turned to water and she fell flat on her face, still running" [p.44]. "Without ceasing to run she appeared to pause" (p. 56, and see p. 49), her face "fixed in that cringing grimace" of placating terror (p. 57). At one point she seems to stand still, helplessly watching "herself run out of her body, out of one slipper" (p. 109, and see p. 77). Other examples occur in the rigid tension of Temple as she cringes against the porch door (p. 76) or at the corner of the kitchen stove (p. 60), lies stiff on the bed as others muse in the darkness beyond (pp. 91, 94–5, and cf. pp. 81, 84), or thrashes impotently on the corn shuck mattress at Ruby's touch (p. 96). Especially as Temple retells it to Horace, that whole evening becomes a nightmare of strange pause in action and of active fantasizing without action. During the frenetic succession of transformations which Temple fantasizes as escapes from Popeye, she lies, seemingly without breathing, paralyzed—at one point she imagines herself dead in a coffin—even when her somehow impersonally frightened skin jerks before Popeye's cold moving touch. Popeye's whole visit in the darkness is an action shrouded, dreamlike, and, of course, incomplete. So too a sense of horrible, helpless lassitude pervades the atmosphere at Miss Reba's when Temple arrives. In the shuttered brothel into which light leaks with "a protracted weariness like a vitiated backwater beyond sunlight" (p. 172), Temple lies frightened, her blood seeping, and listens to the ticking of the clock or the watch, and the sounds outside her room are remote and strangely threatening as in nightmare. Even more pointedly applicable is the rape scene itself. The whole sequence is strange, dazed and still; action seems extremely remote, thus unreal; and sound appears suspended: ". . . it was as though sound and silence had become inverted" (pp. 121–122). Temple sits first in helpless paralysis, "her hands limp and palm-up on her lap" and, as the chapter closes, again lies "thrashing" in one place in the terrified impotence of motion which is non-motion.

The intense, choked horror of nightmare is also conveyed in the "silent" screams of the novel, in the stasis of Temple's long, unuttered "hopeless" cry as she rides with Popeye, "her mouth open and the half chewed mass of bread and meat lying upon her tongue" (p. 169) and in the scream which she finally utters in the rape scene, "like hot silent bubbles into the bright silence" (p. 122). The sense of stifled scream underlies almost all her experiences, until she begins to glory in her Memphis life—at which point she herself becomes part of the nightmare of others, particularly of Horace. And the soundless scream continues into the fiery tableau of Goodwin's lynching in which everything seems "soundless" and dreamlike, including the screams of a man burned by the oil from his exploding can (p. 355). In Faulkner only the castration of Joe Christmas in *Light in August*, with its background sound of the screaming siren like a searing iron upon raw nerves, may be said to evoke equally the feeling of intense paralyzed horror. Indeed it might not be very far wrong to describe the whole experience of agonized, stifled and unresolved terror in the novel as a kind of long soundless scream.

Even the courtroom scene subscribes to the dominant pattern. Once more Temple sits "hands ... motionless, palm-up on her lap," "lax-ankled" in "motionless slippers" above a crowd in which the faces become "white and pallid as the floating bellies of dead fish" (p. 341). In a great gap of silence, Judge Drake's slow progress up the aisle is followed by the "slow gaping of the small white faces" to where Temple sits blank-eyed and immobile (p. 346). The whole scene is like the slow motion of bad dreams; and through it runs the fearful enormity of Temple's lies and the triumph of injustice. Before that enormity Horace himself seems paralyzed into impotence.

The complex of stasis or slow motion and helpless horror which creates the effect of nightmare is also repeatedly conveyed in many smaller scenes and images. For example, it appears in little in the images of cigarette smoke drifting slowly past the viciousness of Popeye's face; in the picture of Ruby's sick child with "its curled hands above its head in the attitude of one crucified" (p. 160); in Temple's remembering the tableau of a group of co-eds poised threateningly about one frightened girl, "their eyes like knives" (p. 182); in Temple's encounter with the rat staring "eye to eye" (p. 111); in the one-handed, empty-faced clock at Miss Reba's which Temple watches to the "faint rasping sounds" of window shades (p. 177); even in the image of the wheel of Gowan's car spinning in the suddenly ominous silence after the accident (p. 45) or in the gruesome slow motion of Red's corpse rolling out of its casket (p. 299).

For that matter, the ostensibly ordinary, like the half-masticated gob of sandwich in the middle of Temple's unuttered scream, functions to accent the nightmare. Outside the central dark dream of *Sanctuary*, men pitch coins in front of the courthouse yard and crowds move about the square, "people buying comfortable things to take home and eat at quiet tables" (p. 197). The "normalcy" of the lives of Belle and Narcissa, which has a kind of horror of its own, helps to sharpen the larger nightmare of which they are unconscious. The somewhat overextended episode of the barber apprentices wandering blindly on the edge of adult evil serves by contrast to point up the dream horror and yet provides a change of pace that helps ultimately to sustain the horror which might otherwise pall. Even the comedy of Red's macabre funeral is a sort of porter-at-the-gate interlude; for the humor, which appears at first sight a departure from the pattern, contains chilling overtones which actually return us to it.

Indeed, the very prevalence of this atmosphere helps partially to clarify what are sometimes regarded as perplexing illogicalities in *Sanctuary*: Why doesn't Temple just escape into the woods at Goodwin's? Why on the trip to Memphis doesn't she slip away from Popeye at the gas station? And why doesn't Horace question Temple at the trial? Although there are others, one answer lies in the nightmare pattern of the book. As in nightmare, helplessly caught in stasis, they cannot do otherwise. The very fact that they do not do these perhaps expected things actually contributes to the atmosphere of horrible dream. The pattern also helps to answer questions about the title. The sense of helpless exposure, without sanctuary, deepens its irony. . . . It is . . . to a universal, cosmic terror that the nightmare of *Sanctuary* is most essentially related.

This view is supported not only by the very recurrence of the images and actions already cited but also by further analysis of some of them and by a series of other examples of the nightmare pattern which are clearly cosmic in implication. And these are moments in the novel which always cry out for attention—moments which, because of the reverberations they set in motion, insist on their large symbolic significance.

Pregnant with such meaning is the heaven-tree outside the jail. . . . The pulsating heaven-tree throws an ominous "splotched shadow" upon the bar-slotted wall behind which lie not only the guilty but the innocent. As in nightmare, the shadow of this heaven symbol "shuddered and pulsed monstrously in scarce any wind" (p. 148). The effect is all stasis and menace. Only an existential fear is inspired by the "heaven" blooms that fall and become dead, slippery smears on the sidewalk. Not cosmic justice and order, but chilling and dark cosmic threat are communicated by Faulkner's handling of the nightmarish heaven-tree.

In the image of the one-armed and therefore slowly moving clock in Temple's room at Miss Reba's, it is as though Faulkner were again pausing to emphasize. This blank-faced symbol, initially an image of quiet dying, of "moribund time" (p. 180), becomes increasingly a chilling reminder of the universal menace. In the night, it becomes the world paralyzed within the cosmic whirl, a "disc suspended in nothingness, the original chaos," and then a "crystal ball holding in its still and cryptic depths the ordered chaos of the intricate and shadowy world upon whose scarred flanks the old wounds whirl onward at dizzy speed into darkness lurking with new disasters" (p. 181). The central suggestion is that of impotent exposure to a huge and enveloping threat. Even the surrounding "nothingness" is not absence of threat but rather a frightening "original chaos." The imagery and diction are full of menace, not only in "chaos," but in "scarred flanks," "wounds," "darkness," "lurking," "disasters." The whirling, "dizzy speed" actually emphasizes the sense of impotence, for it suggests our helplessness, the impossibility of controlling the motion. In this passage, the "ordered chaos" found in the "cryptic depths" of a "shadowy world" offers no comfort. For any notion of real order is dissolved not only by the words "shadowy" and "cryptic" but by the image of the globe whirling without progress in a black universe of constantly "new disasters." Within the larger chaos, any global order is illusory, "shadowy"; and "ordered chaos" is, hopelessly, still chaos. The phrase is frightening in its ironic implications.

The globe reappears as a principal image in Horace Benbow's thought on his return from visiting Temple in the Memphis brothel, and, again, with other images, it helps to convey the terrifying stasis of nightmare in a cosmic dimension. To review the references briefly: In language which echoes significantly that quoted earlier, Horace wishes all the participants, including himself, dead, "cauterized out of the old and tragic flank of the world" (p. 265), and he thinks then "of the expression he had once seen in the eyes of a dead child, and of other dead: the cooling indignation, the shocked despair fading, leaving two empty globes in which the motionless world lurked profoundly in miniature" (p. 266). Like the clock in Temple's room at Miss Reba's, which is also described as "mirrorlike" (p. 180), the vast globe is reflected in the little. Horace also sees the past few days as "a dream filled with all the nightmare shapes it had taken him forty-three years to invent." And, consequently, as he walks toward the house, the insect sounds of the night seem "the chemical agony of a world left stark and dying above the tide-edge of the fluid in which it lived and breathed" (p. 267). In a landscape of nightmare, "The moon stood overhead, but without light; the earth lay beneath, without darkness." After he enters, he thinks of the night sounds as "the friction of the earth on its axis" which may decide "to turn on or to remain forever still: a motionless ball in cooling space, across which a thick smell of honeysuckle writhed like cold smoke" (p. 267).

The images in this interior monologue merge effects of frustrating stasis or near paralysis and of chill and horror on a cosmic scale. The circles of moon and earth stand or lie eerily static, and both microcosmic eye and macrocosmic earth turn into cold, "motionless" globes; a world dying but fixed cannot reach the vanishing source of its life and turns into a "motionless ball." Where there is motion, it is impeded and slow. Rather like paralyzed action, it occurs only with nightmarish difficulty, with "friction" and by "writhing." A sense of strange cold in the spring night helps to create the growing shiver of fear: "Cooling indignation" suggests a series of images at the end of which the empty eyes and their reflected worlds turn completely cold; a chill surrounds the planet over which "cold smoke" moves and around which is only "cooling space." It is the cosmic bad dream. The nightmare which Horace has by his sheltered existence tried to deny for "forty-three years" has come alive. Just before he calls up the memory of the eyes of the dead, he thinks, at first sight somewhat cryptically, "Perhaps it is upon the instant that we realise, admit, that there is a logical pattern to evil, that we die . . ." (pp. 265–266). But in the context, the "logical pattern to evil" is simply the fact of the universal nightmare; when we recognize that everything is "evil," that this is the "logical pattern"—that is, the only pattern which logic permits us to discover and accept—then we must give up. And thus the position of Horace's fantasy at the end of this chapter also becomes explicable, for it is consistent that the sequence should end with his nightmare vision of a female, "bound" and impotent on the flat car, hurtled through a terrifying blackness and a stasis of roaring sound to strange peace as she swings "lazily" and distantly, indifferently, in the sky (p. 268). It is a symbolic moment, pinpointing much that has preceded, for she has passed through the dark nightmare of existence and, to use Horace's earlier phrasing, has been "cauterized out of the old and tragic flank of the world."

Even the old man, Goodwin's father, contributes to the sense of universal nightmare. Blind and deaf, slobbering over his food . . . , the older Goodwin epitomizes, from one point of view, the horror of human decay, the effects of Time. In this way of looking, he becomes man as impotent victim of the cosmic condition. But with his yellow-clotted eyes and tapping stick that seem to pursue the cringing Temple (e.g., pp. 60, 104), he also . . . symbolizes a universal threat. Thus in the heavy silence immediately before the rape, Temple imagines first that she shrieks at the absent "old man with the yellow clots for eyes." But, as she lies helplessly "tossing and thrashing" in one place, she ends by screaming only to two blind and revolting orbs, "the two phlegm-clots above her" (p. 122). Suddenly the disembodied, unseeing and indifferent "clots" expand in dimension and implication; suddenly they also are like globes. They make cosmic this moment of agonizing dread and furious powerlessness. Sightless and disgusting, they offer a dreadful comment on the relationship of the cosmic to man.

In the climactic depiction of the inferno in which Goodwin burns, the paralyzed horror of dreams occurs again; and again the resonances are ultimately vast. At the center of the "circle" of humanity which Horace has entered, the huge flame blazes; "but from the central mass of fire there came no sound at all. It was now indistinguishable, the flames whirling in long and thunderous plumes from a white-hot mass . . ." (p. 355). Horace cannot hear Goodwin. He cannot hear the men. He cannot "hear the fire, though it still swirled upward unabated, as though it were living upon itself, and soundless: a voice of fury like in a dream, roaring silently out of a peaceful void" (p. 355).

"Like in a dream." The sequence is surely as clearly nightmarish as any. The sense of sound cut off, the strange and dreadful deafness of it all, evokes the suppressive effect of nightmare, as if a dreamer's scream can be neither uttered nor heard. The very silence of the auditory images—"thunderous," "voice of fury," and "roaring"—recreates the impossibilities of bad dreams and makes these ordinarily ominous sounds even more threatening. And, as in nightmare, the scene builds an effect of stasis in which powerlessness and enormous dread fuse. Indeed, the moment is one of tremendous and unusually portentous pause, again as though to mark it for significance. It is as if the world had stopped and the tableau of circle around burning center contained all existence. The bonfire becomes the mesmerizing conflagration at the heart of everything. Before it Horace stands immobilized and powerless. Images of the disembodied "voice of fury" (echo of a fearful but now impersonal Voice out of the whirlwind?) and of an ironically "peaceful void" also add huge dimensions to this nightmare. No vast Power intervenes in the barbarous immolation of Goodwin: there is only the frightening "voice" and vast emptiness. The peacefulness of the "void" is, in the context, ironically the equivalent of indifference; it is an extension of the fearful silence of the whole scene.

One generally ignored sequence epitomizes this major experience of paralyzed horror before the nightmare universe: In their fear Miss Reba's vicious poodles express in little the very heart of this feeling in the novel. In a dreamlike tension of "terrific silence," they crouch beneath Temple's bed, static in fright before the possibility of a senseless and murderous chaos—"the flatulent monotony of their sheltered lives snatched up without warning by an incomprehensible moment of terror and fear of bodily annihilation at the very hands [Miss Reba's] which symbolised by ordinary the licensed tranquility of their lives" (p. 186). Snarling and afraid, "crouching there in the dark against the wall" (p. 184) or "crouching against the wall under the bed in that rigid fury of terror and despair" (p. 190), they express, in their impotent fear before threatened annihilation by their ostensibly secure but now erratic universe, the essence of the human nightmare. Although this picture of the cringing animals appears at first sight a casual and unintegrated episode, it is perhaps no coincidence that it occurs at the very center of the book.

It is also striking that the experiences of both Temple and Horace reflect to a degree the symbolic pattern established by Miss Reba's poodles. Horace moves similarly from the secure, if blind, regularity of ordinary living to his exposure, in moments already described, to the nightmare of dark irrationality. Not only his expectation of order and justice in man and man's law, but also his comfortable belief in a just cosmic order is destroyed. . . . Horace somewhat fatuously tries to comfort Ruby with the notion of a polite cosmic order. He tells her that, although God may be "foolish" occasionally, "at least He's a gentleman" (p. 337). It is not, however, very long after that Horace, seeing the signs of spring, thinks, "You'd almost think there was some purpose to it" (p. 350). Significantly, in our last view of Horace, he has retreated into the shell of his conventional home—beneath his bed, so to speak—and, upon Belle's repeated insistence, is about to "lock the back door" (pp. 358, 360), locking behind him the fearful universe. The paralysis inspired by nightmare becomes his permanent condition.

Temple too undergoes a passage from security to nightmare. And between the helpless animals and Temple crouching in a corner of the kitchen or against the porch door of the old mansion, cringing in the bedroom or in the loft, rigid and trembling on chattering shucks or tossing and thrashing beneath the yellow eyes, the parallel is particularly strong. The lines which describe the dogs frozen in fear are immediately and perhaps pointedly followed by a description of Temple "cringing" and "thrashing furiously" but helplessly before Popeye's advance (pp. 190–191). Her journey through the horror impresses the reader, however, a good deal more than it does Temple, whose ultimate response is rather clearly superficial.

The role of the third principal, Popeye, does not, of course, follow the same pattern. . . . Almost all the way through, Popeye is another aspect of the freezing menace of the nightmare. He is the gangsterism of the twenties raised to symbolic power. He thus resembles remarkably the gangster agents of a frighteningly accidental universe in Hemingway's "The Killers"—Faulkner may well have been influenced by the earlier story—and foreshadows, moreover, the cosmic chill evoked by Ionesco's killer in *Tueur Sans Gages*. But . . . in the last chapter . . . as the agent of nightmare becomes the human victim, he contributes significantly to the sense of cosmic irrationality. . . .

Miss Reba's dogs also snap "viciously at one another" (p. 175), and in this they also seem almost to be commenting on the behavior of men within the nightmare world of the novel. Such a picture of men as vicious, snarling and even mad in their relationship emerges from the respectable cruelty of Narcissa, the calculating ruthlessness of Eustace Graham, the aggressive irrationality in the perverted lust of the mob even before the lynching, and the administration of justice in the trial and condemnation of Goodwin; it is reflected in Ruby's belief that Horace, like other men, must be helping her for what he can get out of it (pp. 330–331) and in the old mad woman's judgment that "the good folks live" in jail (p. 326). This complex of human viciousness, irrationality, and injustice becomes part of the total nightmare of the novel; it is itself terrifying and blends easily with the larger horror. And especially in the context of the greater fear, it becomes a most bitter comment on man. But it does not by itself produce that sense of deep horror and paralysis that suffuses the book. The purely human appears the lesser nightmare, a little culpable world within the devastatingly larger immensity.

To see *Sanctuary*, then, only as a criticism of modern society or even as an indignant satire on man's morality is, true as these views are, to miss much of Faulkner's vision. From the shudders of Gothic make-believe, the book moves into the pervasive horrors of authentic nightmare, that sense of clotting stasis, of cringing impotence and fear before threat, which finally dominates the novel. The paralyzed horror of ordinary nightmare, perhaps psycho-sexual in origin, expands and deepens here into the impotent terror before the nightmare of existence. As in great tragedy, the terror is not simply at the human but also at the cosmic condition; and if in *Sanctuary* Faulkner fails to offer the resolutions of great tragedy so that we never wake to real daylight, he also offers no pat solutions or forced redemptions. In later novels, he moves increasingly toward resolutions; and, significantly, images of the constellations begin then to wheel in seasonal order above man's little world. But the truth at this moment in the constant flux of Faulkner's development is the universal dream-horror of existence.

Sanctuary and Frazer's Slain Kings

by Thomas L. McHaney

. . . *Sanctuary* . . . is a brilliantly successful adaptation of Eliot's idea in
The Waste Land, a subtle and fully articulated suffusion of primitive myth
and ritual into a modern fiction.

Faulkner's inspiration seems to be, at least indirectly, Eliot, though his
method differs from Eliot's or Joyce's in *Ullysses*. His source is James G.
Frazer's *The Golden Bough*—most likely the one-volume abridgement,
which Faulkner read in the mid-twenties.[1] His method resembles
Frazer's own design in *The Golden Bough*. And *Sanctuary* borrows title,
opening scene, many elements of characterization, and much plot
development from Frazer's work.

Robert Slabey wrote long ago that "Temple's rape is a perverted
enactment of the rites of the corn spirit as recounted in *The Golden
Bough*."[2] Perhaps he did not suspect—certainly he did not show—that the
identification is a crucial one. *Sanctuary* contains far more than a simple
identification with parts of Frazer. Frazer's concern with Demeter and
the Eleusinian Mysteries is but a portion of a larger story. The legends
and ritual at Eleusis represented only one of hundreds of similar or
similarly intended rites which Frazer compares in order to show a
common source for the gods in the primitive's anxiety about the renewal of food crops and the cosmogonal cycle. In both long and
abridged versions of *The Golden Bough*, Frazer begins his study with the
priest-king who guarded the sacred grove of Diana at Nemi on Lake
Aricia in Italy. He demonstrates how the life and death of this ritual

"*Sanctuary* and Frazer's Slain Kings" by Thomas L. McHaney. Extracted from *Mississippi
Quarterly*, 24 (1971), 223–45. Copyright © 1971 by Mississippi State University. Reprinted by
permission of the publisher.

[1]Carvel Collins, "Faulkner and Anderson: Some Revisions," Talk at the Modern
Language Association Convention, Chicago, December 27, 1967. See also, R. P. Adams,
"The Apprenticeship of William Faulkner," *Tulane Studies in English*, 12 (1962), 151. Collins
says Faulkner read Sherwood Anderson's copy of the one-volume abridgement; Adams says
Phil Stone owned a copy and that Faulkner probably read that. Faulkner did not have a
copy of the book in his library at the time of his death, apparently, but he had access to
libraries at the University of Mississippi, in Memphis, in New Orleans, and in New York,
not to mention Europe, during the period that included the groundwork on *Sanctuary*.

[2]"Faulkner's *Sanctuary*," *Explicator*, 21 (Jan., 1963), Item 45.

figure is mirrored and explained in the lives and deaths of other mythological god-kings—especially Tammuz, Adonis, Osiris, Dionysus, and the impersonator of Zeus in the Eleusinian Mysteries. According to Frazer, the legends and forms of worship surrounding these figures have crucial affinities with all forms of primitive ritual invented to symbolize or to influence seasonal renewal of life. It is this beginning with the King of the Wood out of Frazer, this connection with his avatars in the persons of other god-kings, and this combination of many rituals into one ritual and many gods into one god that Faulkner borrows as he unfolds the perverse Eleusinian Mystery into which Temple Drake is so rudely forced.

It was only in the final version of *Sanctuary*, the revised galley proofs, that Faulkner moved to its prominent position the scene which now opens the novel.[3] This is acknowledged as an excellent scene, and it is strange that Faulkner waited so long to choose it as his first chapter, unless he meant to obscure his source, for it very closely parallels the first few pages of *The Golden Bough*. Kneeling at the woodland spring in the woods near Jefferson, Horace Benbow looks up from drinking to discover Popeye watching him apprehensively. The dark little gangster in the black priestly garb obviously carries a weapon and assumes that Benbow has one, too, and means to use it. He is on his guard. But Horace is not here to usurp the King of the Wood. He has fled the early spring of the Mississippi Delta (16) for the cooler north Mississippi hills of his origin; he has run away from a demanding wife and from the disturbing sensuality of his step-daughter, who entertains her young men in a burgeoning grape-arbor. What he has in his pocket is not a weapon but a book of poetry. A "fishingbird" sings in the shadows. It is May. And this is the beginning of a very black rite of spring.

In order to write this scene the way he did, Faulkner must have gone to Frazer. At the opening of *The Golden Bough* the King of the Wood patrols the sacred grove near the sanctuary of Diana, anxiously awaiting battle with the man who will try to kill him and take his place. Frazer describes the scene of this "strange and recurring tragedy":

> In this sacred grove there grew a certain tree round which at any time of the day, and probably far into the night, a grim figure might be seen to prowl. In his hand he carried a drawn sword, and he kept peering warily about him as if at every instant he expected to be set upon by an enemy. He was a priest and a murderer; and the man for whom he looked was sooner or later to murder him and

---

[3]The first eight lines of the opening represent new material; the rest is paraphrased or revised from the previous version. A look at the manuscript of *Sanctuary*, which shows several differences from the typescript and original galleys, confirms that the elements of Frazer in the final version were already being used.

hold the priesthood in his stead. Such was the rule of the sanctuary.[4]

Frazer pictures the scene as it "may have been witnessed by a belated wayfarer" such as Benbow: ". . . the background of forest showing black and jagged against a lowering and stormy sky, the sighing of the wind in the branches, the rustle of the withered leaves under foot, the lapping of the cold water on the shore, and in the foreground, pacing to and fro, now in twilight and now in gloom, a dark figure with a glitter of steel at the shoulder whenever the pale moon, riding clear of the cloud-rack, peers down at him through the matted boughs" (Frazer, p. 2).

Frazer paints an autumnal scene, while Faulkner converts his to springtime, and for a very good reason that is perfectly in accord with Frazer, but the physical descriptions in both cases are very close:

The Golden Bough	Sanctuary
. . . forest showing black and jagged against a lowering and stormy sky. . . . (Frazer, p. 2)	. . . above a black, jagged mass of trees, the house lifted its stark square bulk against the failing sky. [6]

There can be little doubt that Faulkner's "sanctuary" refers to Diana's shrine at Nemi or that he borrowed the word from Frazer, who uses that word eleven times in the first seven pages of *The Golden Bough* to describe it. The Arician grove was peopled with a various crew. Diana of course was there. She bore the title of Vesta and shared her "forest sanctuary" with "Egeria, the nymph of the clear water," an embodiment of the pure spring which welled out of nearby rocks and from which the Roman vestals fetched water to "wash the temple" (Frazer, pp. 4–5). Diana's consort was Virbius, whom some identified with the chaste and fair youth Hippolytus; he was supposed to have been killed when his chariot was wrecked beside the sea, but some believed the goddess had rescued him and given him sanctuary in the grove. On his behalf, reflecting the bolting of his horses in the accident, horses were excluded from the precincts of the temple (Frazer, p. 5). A proverbial expression—"There are many Manii at Aricia"—was interpreted to mean, according to Frazer, that "there were many ugly and deformed people" at the sanctuary (Frazer, pp. 6–7). There was a perpetually tended fire. And the lives of the successive kings, writes Frazer, "were in a manner bound up with a certain tree in the grove, because so long as that tree was uninjured they were safe from attack" (Frazer, p. 10).

[4]Sir James G. Frazer, *The Golden Bough*, 1 Volume, abridged (New York: Macmillan, 1951), p. 1. The opening of the first volume of the complete *Golden Bough* is the same. This edition is a reprint of the original 1922 abridgement.

Popeye's execution on the gallows supports his association with *The Golden Bough* through Eliot's reference to "The Hanged God of Frazer" in the notes to *The Waste Land*.[5] But he is also clearly modeled on the King of the Wood, with the twist of inversion applied. He keeps armed vigil in the grove outside the Old Frenchman's Place, and well he might, for he has caused the protective tree to be cut down in order to keep automobiles out of the sanctuary (22) (though, like Hades, with whom he also may be identified, he drives a canary-colored car [326]); there are no horses in this grove either, as Horace notes just after he steps across the felled tree: "no mark of hoof" (5). Before leading Benbow to the house, Popeye spits into the spring where Horace had sought a drink. He shuns a shortcut through the woods because he is afraid of the trees (5). His face resembles a mask "carved into two simultaneous expressions" (3), suggesting Frazer's identification of Diana's consort Virbius with Janus, the two-headed god of portals (Frazer, pp. 190–91); the identification is amplified by the manner in which Popeye frequently leans in doorways to stare at Ruby or Temple (7, 8, 55, 121). Popeye ushers Benbow into the midst of a collection of "crimps and spungs and feebs" (8), underworld cant for the kind of "ugly and deformed" people said to be at Aricia. One of these, the fawning, protective half-wit Tommy, tells Benbow that Popeye has killed a dog (21), the animal sacred to Diana and crowned at her annual festival (Frazer, p. 4). Tommy himself is dog-like and the animal is perhaps his totem: slavering, he repeats the expression "I be a dog" and "I be dog" (21) as he tells the story which prefigures his own death also at Popeye's hands. There is a kind of perpetual fire in the ruined house, tended by Ruby Lamar, who also makes several trips a day to the spring for water, a fact that astonishes Temple. The debauched Virginia Gentleman, Gowan Stevens, will play Hippolytus here, wrecking his car against the tree Popeye has had felled. He will be identified with the pig, the animal that figured in Demeter's worship at Eleusis. Popeye reacts violently to an owl which flies in his face (6), demonstrating his disharmony with nature and, perhaps, a female sex totem,[6] as Frazer notes in a relevant context (pp. 798–99), while the "fishingbird" to which

<hr>

[5]Slabey's 1963 *Explicator* note connects Popeye and Hermes, an identification that holds up and fits easily into the context of the allusions to Frazer discussed in this essay.

[6]The identification of these animals as totems is not as far-fetched as it may at first sound, particularly in view of Faulkner's later use of similar material in *As I Lay Dying* and *Go Down, Moses*: Vardaman Bundren's confusion of his mother and the fish; the pairing of Boon and Lion, Sam and the bear. Cf. Frazer, p. 798: "Now, when men's lives are thus supposed to be contained in certain animals, it is obvious that the animals can hardly be distinguished from the men, or the men from the animals. If my brother John's life is in a bat, then . . . the bat is my brother . . . and, on the other hand, John is in a sense a bat. . . . Similarly, if my sister Mary's life is in an owl, then the owl is my sister and Mary is an owl."

Benbow calls so much attention is a male sex totem as well as a probable reference to the related Fisher King of *The Waste Land*.[7]

This is a wasteland scene, reinforced when Temple and Gowan reach the Old Frenchman's Place. It is "set in a ruined lawn, surrounded by abandoned grounds and fallen outbuildings. But nowhere was any sign of husbandry . . . only a gaunt weather-stained ruin in a sombre grove" (47). The aptly named Temple and her unchivalrous companion are at first spoiled avatars of Hippolytus and his consort in Diana's grove, the virgin Artemis, though they will play other roles in the masquerade. Both are cruelly innocent, and evidently chaste, despite efforts to appear otherwise. Tommy remarks Temple's chastity (and barrenness) when he regards her slim figure and says, "He aint laid no crop by yit, has he?" (47), an expression, under the circumstances, which is a pointed reference to the role played by the Demeter-surrogate in the Eleusinian Mysteries. Temple is a kind of unholy innocent, a tease and a flirt, chaste in body if not in spirit until her brutal rape. Like Diana the virgin huntress, she is always pictured running (31, 41, 50, etc.).

Horace and Temple cross paths at the sanctuary, though they do not meet. Their different reactions to events which follow are explained by the contrasted motives which have sent each on a May journey. Temple is out for sensual adventures, misusing the opportunity offered by the colorful spring ritual of the special college train to the Ole Miss-Mississippi State baseball game, an event she imagines in appropriately distorted terms:

> thinking of the pennant-draped train already in Starkville; of the colorful stands; the band, the yawning glitter of the bass horn; the green diamond dotted with players, crouching, uttering short, yelping cries like marsh-fowl disturbed by an alligator, not certain of where the danger is, motionless, poised, encouraging one another with short meaningless cries, plaintive, wary and forlorn. (43)

Once she is initiated into the worst she can experience, she discovers an apparently insatiable appetite for sex and evil. Horace on the other hand flees the Dionysiac symbols of the year's renewal in the fertile delta:

> From my window I could see the grape arbor. . . . That's why we know nature is a she; because of that conspiracy between female flesh and female season. So each spring I could watch the reaffirmation of the old ferment hiding the hammock; the green-snared

[7]Horace's Carolina Wren makes the identification possible; the "hunting of the wren" is also discussed by Frazer as a ritual paralleling the slaying of the god-king of the fertility cult (Frazer, pp. 621–23). Appropriately, Horace is referred to as a "bird" (7). In the same context, see the way Tommy and his dog are linked.

promise of unease . . . in late May, in the twilight, her—Little
Belle's—voice would be like the murmur of the wild grape itself.
(13–14)

His fate, like Temple's, is excess; he encounters in the hills a debauched
sexuality and criminality that he cannot handle at all. What Horace flees,
Temple seeks; what revolts Horace, attracts Temple. The man who stole
into the sacred wood and defeated the old King of the Wood became
Diana's new consort. His act was a symbolic gesture betokening the
death of the old year and the birth of the new. But Horace never ac-
complishes this. The action takes place in Eliot's "depraved May," not in
the season of rebirth. The entanglement of Horace's and Temple's fate-
lines ensnares several outsiders—Tommy, Goodwin, and Red—while
the inept middle-aged lawyer and the bored corrupt college girl resume
their former meaningless lives when all is finished. They seem unchanged, but the worlds to which they return are unredeemed and dead.

In *The Golden Bough* Frazer, as noted, shows that the ritual surrounding
the King of the Wood resembles similar rites of renewal from many
cultures and many times, especially, however, the tales and rituals
associated with Demeter and Zeus, Isis and Osiris, Astarte and Tammuz,
Aphrodite and Adonis. Frazer believes all these deities are vegetation
gods and embodiments of the corn, or grain; they are worshipped
similarly because their legends come from similar sources in human
history. He constantly draws parallels between these mythological characters, though he never quite creates the paradigm, or Monomyth, as
Joseph Campbell has called it in *The Hero with a Thousand Faces.*[8] In
Sanctuary, Faulkner is doing almost the same thing as Frazer; that is, he
establishes the same parallels between the characters of his novel as
Frazer does between the gods and goddesses with whom he deals. Most
of the men around Temple Drake carry associations with the consorts of
Diana, Demeter, Isis, or Aphrodite. Most of the women in the novel—
Temple, Ruby Lamar, Narcissa Benbow, Horace's wife Belle, Miss Reba,
and so on—are identified with the goddesses themselves, or with important related figures out of Frazer.

The Demeter context is one of the most important, and perhaps the
one which is most meaningful for Faulkner; throughout his career, the
corn goddess and her daughters were among Faulkner's favorite sources
of allusion. Demeter (who with Persephone and Kore is often thought of
as a tri-une goddess) and her followers initiated brides and bridegrooms
into the secrets of the marriage bed. She had no husband of her own, but
she bore a son to her brother, Zeus. Her daughter Persephone was
carried off to the underworld by Hades, or Pluto, in his golden car. The

---

[8]The question of Frazer's accuracy as an anthropological researcher or theorist, which
has come under fire in recent years, is not at issue here, since we are not dealing in
archetypes but with a patent case of literary borrowing.

swineherd Eubuleus, whose pigs fell into the pit of darkness at the time, witnessed the abduction and told the goddess. Wearing a veil, Demeter wandered in search of her daughter, coming in the course of time to Eleusis. There she took Demophoön, son of King Celeus, and held him over a glowing fire to purge him of his mortality, though the child's mother, misunderstanding the ritual, stopped her and denied the boy eternal life. She also is supposed to have given the secrets of the culture of the olive to a nearby people. Demeter's legends helped to explain the core of the Eleusinian Mysteries which grew out of her worship at Eleusis. Like all the ritual which Frazer discusses in *The Golden Bough*, the rites at Eleusis were symbolic acts to insure the renewal of the land. They included ritual copulation between a surrogate of the goddess and a priest-king who impersonated Zeus. The priest-king rendered himself impotent by the deliberate application of hemlock. The conclusion of the Mysteries, which followed this symbolic copulation, was the dramatic display of a reaped ear of corn to which the goddess was said to have given birth.[9]

We have seen how the opening of *Sanctuary* identifies the Old Frenchman's Place with the sanctuary of Diana at Nemi. Diana and Egeria (the embodiment of the spring) were both, like Demeter, important to childbirth. In this context, Ruby Lamar's sickly child is a piece of wasteland irony. Temple (as Diana and Demeter) holds on to it, but as a means of protecting herself, not out of any concern for its well-being (64). She whispers despairingly, "He's going to die" (73), though the baby is perpetually kept near the stove (to keep off the rats). Demeter's attempt to confer immortality on Demophoön (as well as the similar story Frazer tells about Isis) likewise figures in the antics of Popeye's incendiary grandmother, who cryptically justifies the fires she keeps setting by crying, "Them bastards are trying to get him" (364, 368).

The conclusion of the Eleusinian Mysteries was the ritual intercourse between the impotent priest-king and the Demeter figure. As Frazer describes it, "The torches having been extinguished, the pair descended into a murky place. . . . After a time the hierophant reappeared, and in a blaze of light silently exhibited to the assembly a reaped ear of corn, the fruit of the divine marriage" (Frazer, p. 165). A similar rite at Athens, Frazer also records on the same page, united the wine-god, Dionysus,[10] with the queen; the act there took place in the "old official residence of

[9]Frazer, pp. 456–62, 437, 165, etc. The wanderings and deeds of Isis are similar (cf. Frazer, p. 423). Demeter's legend is recounted in Bulfinch, too, of course, a copy of which Faulkner owned at the time of his death.

[10]Associations with Dionysus in *Sanctuary* are legion, if in a minor key, through Popeye and Goodwin's involvement with bootlegging. Benbow's flight from the grape arbor and Gowan's devotion to the art of drinking seem related; and even the antics of Uncle Bud, the little boy who visits Miss Reba and filches so much beer he becomes sick, may parody the Dionysian mode.

the King, known as the Cattle-stall" (Frazer, p. 165). Temple is raped by the impotent priest-murderer Popeye in the corn crib near the empty cattle stalls which serves as privies (104). The drama is completed only at Lee Goodwin's trial when Eustace Graham dramatically displays the stained corn cob that was used in the act (340).

The Demeter story is invoked in another way through Gowan Stevens, who is linked with the pigs that figured in the worship of the goddess. Twice Temple calls him pig (41) and Popeye says he looks "like a damn hog with its throat cut" (51) after his fight with Van. These associations provide transition to an important parallel in the legends of Osiris, for, as Frazer notes, "the killing of the pig was the annual representation of the killing of Osiris, just as the throwing of the pigs into the caverns at the Thesmophoria was an annual representation of the descent of Persephone into the lower world" (Frazer, p. 551). The legend of Osiris and his consort Isis, like the allusions to Diana and Virbius and Demeter and Zeus, plays an important role in *Sanctuary*. Besides Gowan, Lee Doodwin is clearly identified with Osiris, in whose honor the Egyptians performed rites of immolation (Frazer, p. 439). Osiris is said to have been the first in his country to "tread the grapes." Leaving the government of Egypt to his wife, Isis, he "travelled over the world, diffusing the blessings of civilization." Eventually plotted against by his brother Set, he was tricked into a coffin and his whereabouts was hidden from Isis, who wandered the world, veiled like Demeter, trying to secure his freedom (Frazer, pp. 420–45). Like Demeter, in the course of her travels Isis attempted to confer immortality upon a child by holding him over a fire. Goodwin's bootlegging associates him with the treading of the grape. During his army service, Goodwin has wandered the world (332–33). He is shut up and his whereabouts is kept from Ruby, who must travel the country trying to find him and arrange his freedom. Like Isis and Demeter, Ruby wears a veil when she enlists Benbow's aid (he "could not remember when he had seen one before, when women ceased to wear veils" [138]). Ruby keeps her sickly child beside the stove.

"Red," the young man whom Popeye secures to be his surrogate with Temple, is also a type of the red-headed Egyptian corn-god (whose hair represented the tassels of the new grain).[11] Osiris' entrapment occurred at a party given by his brother Set; "when they were all drinking and . . . making merry he [Set] brought in the coffer [*sic*] and jestingly promised to give it to the one whom it should fit exactly" (Frazer, p. 422). At Red's funeral, after the drinking is underway, a "woman in red" starts yelling about the proprietor of the speakeasy: "Put the son of a bitch in a coffin. See how he likes it" (297). Osiris was killed on the seventeenth of the month, the same day as Red (361; see Frazer, p. 422). As corn spirit,

[11]See Frazer, pp. 439, 551, for immolation of red-haired men in corn rites.

Osiris was sometimes buried in effigy (a figure made of dried corn, or grain); after a short interval, the effigy was exhumed and "the corn would be found to have sprouted from the body of Osiris, and this . . . would be hailed as an omen, or rather as the cause, of the growth of the crops. The corn-god produced the corn from himself; he gave his own body to feed the people; he died that they might live" (Frazer, p. 437). At Red's funeral, the coffin is knocked over and the body falls out; when they raise it up, they find that a "wreath came too, attached to him by a hidden end of a wire driven into his cheek" (299). The omen of promise is appropriately artificial in Faulkner's novel.[12]

A further word on the ritual of Red's funeral is in order to show how Faulkner, like Frazer, goes beyond the outlines of the main mythological stories to pick up less significant and often more contemporaneous rites parallel to the main theme. The wild underworld wake, for instance, seems to come directly from Frazer's section on "burying the carnival" (Frazer, pp. 350–57), a burlesque funeral that had the same religious function as the slaying of the god-kings. Frazer recounts a number of instances of drinking, fighting, and mockery, of which the following is a characteristic example: ". . . the hymn of the Carnival is now thundered out, after which, amid a deafening roar, aloe leaves and cabbages are whirled aloft and descend impartially on the heads of the just and the unjust, who lend fresh zest to the proceedings by engaging in a free fight" (Frazer, p. 352). After "Nearer My God to Thee," "That Haven of Rest," and "Sonny Boy," the mourners at Red's funeral riot and the "floral offerings" fly (299). The host has said, "I might have knowed somebody'd have to turn it into a carnival" (294). With similar intent— that is, to follow Frazer and to support his central mythic material with lesser identifications—Faulkner stages Goodwin's death with reference to the midsummer fires. His immolation occurs on June 22, the summer solstice.[13] Ignorantly, Horace Benbow has just said, "It does last . . . Spring does. You'd almost think there was some purpose to it" (350). But the spring season has ended with the coming of the summer solstice and its "celebration" (cf. Frazer, pp. 720–32).

Popeye, as shown, is identified at the beginning of the novel with the

---

[12]Red, the woman in red, and *Ruby* Lamar may be connected through Frazer, too. He theorizes that many of the pairs of gods and goddesses had names with identical roots and identical meanings: "Jupiter and Juno . . . Dianus and Diana, or Janus and Jana . . . are merely duplicates of each other, their names and their functions being in substance and origin identical. With regard to their names, all four of them come from the same Aryan root, *DI*, meaning 'bright,' which occurs in the names of the corresponding Greek deities, Zeus and his old female consort Dione" (Frazer, pp. 190–91).

[13]The trial opens on June 20 (322–23); Temple testifies the second day and the jury renders a verdict (334–49); that night, shortly after midnight, the mob takes him from jail and burns him alive (353).

King of the Wood. Whatever apprehension he has about Benbow's advent (and it becomes ironic, even to Popeye, who refers to the book in the lawyer's pocket and says, "Like he would jump me with a book or something. Take me for a ride with the telephone directory" [116]), Red's competition, or Goodwin's testimony at the trial, Popeye will not be usurped. Ultimately responsible for all the deaths in the book, including his own, when he will not act to clear himself of the one crime he did not commit, Popeye will not be replaced either. Besides this inverted association with Virbius, Diana's consort, however, and the brief identification with Hades abducting Persephone in a golden car, he too resembles Osiris. He is arrested for the murder of an Alabama policeman on June 17 (361), the day he murdered Red and numerically a reference to the date of Osiris' death. He is apprehended and put to death in August, apparently aged twenty-eight (born on Christmas, 1900 [363]), a reference to the traditional age of Osiris at his death (Frazer, p. 422).[14] Finally, Popeye's association with Memphis, Tennessee, was a natural link to Osiris' association with the like-named Egyptian city, and conceivably part of Faulkner's inspiration for the use of the parallels.[15]

Temple begins as a sort of virgin Artemis, consort to Gowan's Hippolytus, and becomes a surrogate of Diana and Demeter-Persephone, consort to Popeye in his roles as Virbius and Hades. Her hallucination, in which she imagines "I had on a veil like a bride, and I was crying because I was dead . . . No; it was because they had put shucks in the coffin" (263), links her with Isis and Osiris. Ruby carries many of these same associations: she plays Diana at the grove, where she is also vestal to the temple of the sanctuary, fetching water and tending the perpetual fire; she plays Demeter with her sickly child; and Isis to Goodwin's Osiris. Miss Reba is similarly linked to Frazer: she operates an ironic

[14]At the time of his execution, Popeye fills twelve spaces marked out on the floor of his cell; he lays out cigarette butts as he counts down to the time of his August execution. We do not know the date, but given the specific associations with other real dates from Frazer in the novel, his actions at least point to August 13, Diana's day (Frazer, p. 6).

[15]In the strangely surreal account of Popeye's childhood, the fires his grandmother kindles to keep the "bastards" from "getting him" connect him with Osiris, and the cryptic emphasis on olive oil (365–66) may play back to Diana's association with the sacred olive (Frazer, p. 8) and Demeter's lament under the olive tree (Frazer, p. 457).

Robert Cantwell (*Nation*, 15 Feb. 1958) has shown that Faulkner modeled his character and drew his character's name from a Memphis gangster of the period named Popeye Pumphrey. Pumphrey, in turn, had come by the nickname in his youth. But Faulkner has another reference, tipped also by the emphasis on olive oil. Faulkner added this episode to the revised *Sanctuary* in 1930 (Massey, pp. 197–98, 201–02 [*See* Bibliography.—Ed.]). Elzie C. Segar's popular comic strip, "Thimble Theatre," had introduced the now-famous Popeye on January 17, 1929, and within a few weeks he had attained great popularity. The sailor replaced Ham Gravy as Olive Oyl's perpetual suitor. Coulton Waugh, *The Comics* (New York: Macmillan, 1947), p. 195. The comic dialogue between Popeye's grandmother and the chauffeur clearly resembles the humor of Segar's strip.

sanctuary filled with vestals; she bedecks a pair of dogs (Diana's sacred animals), who are comic surrogates of the madam and her dead consort, Mr. Binford.[16] Like Isis, she might be called "The Lady of Beer" (Frazer, p. 444; cf. *Sanctuary*, pp. 171, 302). Even Narcissa Benbow is linked with these vegetation gods and goddesses in a pointed manner: Horace thinks of her as "living a life of serene vegetation like perpetual corn or wheat in a sheltered garden instead of a field" (127).

In a fiction beneath the fiction where the characters impersonate gods who were killed or abducted then resurrected or returned to the upper world, *Sanctuary* depicts a wasteland without rebirth. Popeye has not made himself temporarily impotent, like the hierophant who impersonated Zeus in the Eleusinian Mysteries, he is really impotent. Temple is subjected to real rape, not symbolic copulation, and the object involved is a rat-gnawed corn-cob; she does not give birth to the newly reaped corn. Apparently she prefers the underworld to the world above. Persephone fasted during most of her sojourn below, but as she was leaving she was tricked into eating a pomegranate seed, thereby putting herself in Hades' power. He could compel her return to the underworld each year for a season (Frazer, p. 457). At Miss Reba's,[17] Temple fasts briefly, but eventually she eats heartily (275). Her periodic damnation seems assured, as we see in the final scene of the novel: she readies herself for the "season of rain and death" by applying makeup (380), as if for a date. Here in the land of the living, as at the trial, she is lifeless. Only in the "dead" world of Miss Reba and Popeye has she shown vitality.

Temple is not alone in being corrupted, however; everyone is touched in one way or another. As there is no redemptor in *The Sound and the Fury* who harries Hell and ascends with the suffering to paradise, and no heroic leader of the absurd quest in *As I Lay Dying* who can unite the selfishly divided family, in *Sanctuary* there is no virile young priest-king who appears to reclaim the land from its barrenness and restore life to the world. Ignorant of Temple's fate after he has abandoned her, Gowan writes Narcissa, *"I have injured no one save myself by my folly"* (154); yet even he knows better, for as he left the Old Frenchman's Place, he was "whispering Jesus Christ to himself in a kind of despair" (101), like a consciously failed Grail knight. Narcissa lives her life of "serene vegetation," and tries to preserve her innocence by arranging the betrayal of

[16]The name of Miss Reba's consort, Mr. Binford, is probably a local joke for Faulkner. Lloyd T. Binford, born in Duck Hill, Miss., in 1866, was by the 1920s an active voice in Memphis civic life. In that period he became one of the most notorious censors of films and other forms of entertainment in America. From 1928 until his death he was chairman of the Memphis board of censors. (See *Time*, August 13, 1945, p. 20, and his obituary, *Time*, Sept. 10, 1956, p. 90.)

[17]Slabey notes that Miss Reba's surname, Rivers, suggests her hellish connections, and that Temple's drinking of gin parallels the drinking of Lethe's waters.

Horace and his client, Goodwin. Horace fails and returns to his wife and step-daughter, a situation which includes the humiliation of carrying dripping boxes of shrimp to his wife each Friday, a wretched perversion of a once meaningful religious act.[18] This is such an inescapable symbol for him that he persists in seeing the fallen blossoms of the heaven tree in the Jefferson jail yard as reminders of the dripping shrimp. Popeye shoots the harmless Tommy like a dog; he kills Red, and his associates give Red a mockery of a funeral. Goodwin will not defend himself, nor will Popeye. All die absurdly. At his execution the dark gangster becomes Eliot's "Hanged God of Frazer," but all he is concerned about is whether his hair is brushed back or not. The hope of the future is expressed in Ruby's sickly child, appallingly like the baby Popeye, even if it survives: a wretched second coming.

The Tiresias who views and suffers all this is Horace Benbow. In the opening scene, as he kneels at the woodland pool, he may be identified with his sister, Narcissa, through the vain creature whose name she bears. Like a Prufrock, too, Horace, whose hair is thin, has seen everything already. He has begun by running away from "that curious small flesh which he had not begot and in which appeared to be vatted delicately some seething sympathy with the blossoming grape" (200). But when Temple has told him her story, he confuses her and Little Belle and then himself enters into the female experience. He is appalled, we know: he thinks that every witness to any of this, every one who has heard Temple's story even, including himself, should be exterminated, "cauterised out of the old and tragic flank of the world," as if to eliminate such knowledge of evil would purge the world of that evil (265). He leaves Miss Reba's and returns directly to Jefferson and his house, where he takes up Little Belle's picture, responds to the voluptuous face, and vomits. At that moment he recalls the rest of Temple's impressions, which he has held in suspension during the journey home, and her experiences become his:

[18]There is no evidence in *Sanctuary* or *Sartoris*, where she also appears, that Belle is a Roman Catholic, but the Friday shrimp point to ritual fasting clearly enough. Belle's love of "shrimps" applies with obvious irony to Horace, as well, a fact which Little Belle notes (15).

At the end of his part in the novel, back with Belle, Horace calls his step-daughter on the telephone. As he waits to make the call, "He began to say something out of a book he had read: 'Less oft is peace. Less oft is peace,' he said" (359). The quotation is from Shelley's poem "To Jane: The Recollection." The first stanza, though its subject is not quite right, speaks of a world like the one depicted in the final pages of *Sanctuary*: "the Earth has changed its face, / A frown is on the Heaven's brow." The last stanza, beginning "We paused beside the pools that lie / Under the forest boughs," carries us back to the opening of the novel. The last two lines, from which Horace quotes, mirror his state of mind in the romantic terms he always uses (in *Sartoris*, too): "Less oft is peace in Shelley's mind,/Than calm in waters seen."

> . . . he gave over and plunged forward and struck the lavatory and
> leaned upon his braced arms while the shucks set up a terrific
> uproar beneath her thighs. Lying with her head lifted slightly, her
> chin depressed like a figure lifted down from a crucifix, she
> watched something black and furious go roaring out of her pale
> body. (268)

Fleeing the Delta, Horace had only wanted a "hill to lie on" (17), but he is
ten years past the christological age of 33 and he is not the stuff martyrs
are made of, anyway, so his hill will not be some Calvary. Also relevant is
Frazer's discussion of the Beltane fires, kindled on May 1 in the high-
lands of Scotland (Frazer, pp. 715–20), rites connected with the Midsummer fires in which Goodwin perishes; yet Horace will not suffer
immolation, either, although he is threatened with it momentarily (355).
His movement from the fertile Mississippi Delta to the north Mississippi
hills is the movement of the mythology in the background of the tale: it
goes from Egypt and Osiris to the Alban Hills of Italy, where the King of
the Wood kept his lonely vigil at Diana's sanctuary. Horace may have the
experience, but he misses the meaning; he gains nothing, achieves
nothing.

Sanctuary chronicles nothing but meaningless deaths, unregenerated
lives. Frazer has done just the opposite, and the ending of *The Golden
Bough* linked the meaningful patterns of the present with the meaningful
patterns of the past: "The temple of the sylvan goddess, indeed, has
vanished and the King of the Wood no longer stands sentinel over the
Golden Bough. But Nemi's woods are still green, and as the sunset fades
above them in the west, there comes to us, borne on the swell of the
wind, the sound of the church bells of Aricia ringing the Angelus. *Ave
Maria!* Sweet and solemn they chime out from the distant town and die
lingeringly away across the wide Campagnan marshes. *Le roi est mort, vive
le roi! Ave Maria!*" (Frazer, p. 827). But the one-volume abridgement of *The
Golden Bough* appeared in the same year as Eliot's *The Waste Land* and
those words from an earlier time did not have the same ring any more.
Temple has lain on the corn-shuck mattress awaiting her fate "like an
effigy on an ancient tomb" (84); she feels as isolated as if she were
"bound to a church steeple" (190); and, in Horace's vision, she lies "like
a figure lifted down from a crucifix" (268). At the end, in the autumn,
surveying her past in a mirror as she regards that "face in miniature
sullen and discontented and sad" (379), yawning her boredom, Temple
sits in a different grove with her father (like Osiris and Zeus, he's a judge).
"[A]cross the pool and the opposite semicircle of trees . . . the dead
tranquil queens in stained marble mused" and the sky lay "prone and
vanquished in the embrace of the season of rain and death" (380). This is
the way the world ends when it is not renewed by acts celebrating the

fertility of nature. In the petty gangsters, bored collegians, sheltered
Southern matrons, garrulous and ineffectual lawyers of his place and
time, Faulkner found a perfect cast to perform the inefficacious rite. The
Kind of the Wood is dead. The queen-goddesses are lost and profaned.
The sacred oak itself has been felled. And even the substituted Catholic
ritual has become an obscene and emasculating chore. What Faulkner
dealt with in *Sanctuary* was hardly a cheap idea, and it is profoundly
handled. . . .

The Profaned Temple

by David Williams

... *Sanctuary* is undoubtedly the most horrorific, and perhaps the most despairing, narrative Faulkner ever published. It is difficult to doubt, by story's end, that its female protagonist has substance in a cosmic and inhuman dimension: the repetition of the three variants of "dying" in the concluding sentence, the final widening perspective which opens out from Temple through the marble queens onto an all-encompassing season of doom, and the weight of the story's final word falling on "death" all contribute markedly to a tone of cosmic annihilation. Each of the men who figures importantly in the novel's opening scene at the Old Frenchman place has by now met with violent destruction or utter defeat while the focal point of the completed action sits in sullen discontent in Paris, pruning herself in a small vanity mirror, at the same time that the narrator is linking her to powers which would seem to lie beyond her, causes which are large enough to be allied with Earth herself.

That Temple's symbolic attributes are no mere fortuitous circumstance nor a late and gratuitous addition to the narrative seem to be borne out by certain recurrent images, the most notable of which is the penultimate clause, "the dead tranquil queens in stained marble mused" (p. 380). Much earlier in the story, while Temple yet maintains a fascinated equipoise between inviolacy and violation, she is described as lying on the chattering cornshuck mattress, "her hands crossed on her breast and her legs straight and close and decorous, like an effigy on an ancient tomb" (p. 84). The "effigy" is of course identified with "the dead tranquil queens in stained marble," who in turn participate, symbolically at least, in the "cosmic season of rain and death." Nonetheless, Faulkner can hardly be said to be creating only mood by his imagery (although he does so very skilfully). He is also representing the ancient death goddess in maternal form: in the feminine season which holds the masculine sky "prone and vanquished"; in the stained marble statues

"The Profaned Temple" (editor's title) is extracted from *Faulkner's Women: The Myth and the Muse* by David Williams (Montreal and London: McGill–Queen's University Press, 1977), pp. 129–30, 136–53. Copyright © 1977 by McGill-Queen's University Press. Reprinted by permission of the publisher.

which muse above the gloom of the trees; in the figure of an earthly woman who presides indifferently and without regard over the demise of her would-be lovers and over the wane of the moribund year.

... On a simply popular level, *Sanctuary* appears to fulfil a public appetite for tales of sex and violence. Indeed, sexuality seems throughout this novel to be the mother of violence, in both act and progeny. The story hinges on a shockingly brutal rape; the fruits of the act are murder, lynching, and execution. So far, there is nothing to indicate that these events are more than the stock ingredients of a lurid bestseller. But when Horace listens to Temple's account of the night leading to her violation, his response illuminates the wider meaning of a number of incidents in the narrative. Returning from Memphis late in the night,

> He walked quietly up the drive, beginning to smell the honeysuckle from the fence. The house was dark, still, as though it were marooned in space by the ebb of all time. The insects had fallen to a low monotonous pitch, everywhere, nowhere, spent, as though the sound were the chemical agony of a world left stark and dying above the tide-edge of the fluid in which it lived and breathed. The moon stood overhead, but without light; the earth lay beneath, without darkness. He opened the door and felt his way into the room and to the light. The voice of the night—insects, whatever it was—had followed him into the house; he knew suddenly that it was the friction of the earth on its axis, approaching that moment when it must decide to turn on or to remain forever still: a motionless ball in cooling space, across which a thick smell of honeysuckle writhed like cold smoke. (pp. 266–67)

The cataclysmic imagery of his despairing thought is most significant in its relation to his sexual revulsion. For the scent of honeysuckle evokes in him the same suffocating sensation of female sexuality, of cloying fertility, that it does in another of Faulkner's anti-vital intellectuals, Quentin Compson. But where Quentin dreams only of a private, etherealized incestuous destruction in response to honeysuckle, Horace envisions an entire world destroyed and wound in the writhing coils of sexual provocation. The ball of earth, which has become masculine for the moment in his agonized mind, is seen as finally burned away by feminine heat, motionless, dead now and cooling, though held still in the embrace of an insatiable power. All the concrete symbols of Benbow's nighttime world coalesce to produce his prophecy of cosmic annihilation: the moon rides darkly overhead, the goddess in her waning and destructive aspect; the furious seethe of insect sound drops off, life stranded and spent on a shore from which the moon-driven tide has ebbed. Ephemeral, then, as gnats and no more than insect-sized, the dependent world of masculine life is conceived as being at the mercy of a dominant and perhaps capricious goddess. So Temple Drake, who has functioned as the catalyst of this male response, is more vitally connected to an awesome force.

Nevertheless, the dying ebb of insect sound still carries for Horace the capacity of choice. Proleptically, he imagines that before the globe ceases to spin on its axis, it voluntarily succumbs to its own inertia and friction: it longs (Darl Bundren-like) to abandon the terrible effort of motion. The male principle thus relinquishes, of its own accord, its source of life in the daemonic archetype. Horace, as even his name suggests the book-learned man, would call that decision a legitimate response to evil: "Perhaps it is upon the instant that we realise, admit, that there is a logical pattern to evil, that we die, he thought, thinking of the expression he had once seen in the eyes of a dead child, and of other dead: the cooling indignation, the shocked despair fading, leaving two empty globes in which the motionless world lurked profoundly in miniature" (p. 266). Death without the indignation and despair of evil, he implies, is better than life intertwined with vice. His dictional choices, however, expose in "logical pattern" and "shocked despair" his own blighted roots; he is a rational idealist who must impute his own logical absolut-ism to evil as abstract order rather than accept the indissoluble unity of good—bad, life—death, virtue—vice, in the very tissue of living.

Evil is more to Horace than an aberration from a moral code; it is a function of the engendering flesh. His very reflection on evil is prompted indirectly by the sight of two figures standing face to face in an alley, " the man speaking in a low tone unprintable epithet after epithet in a caressing whisper, the woman motionless before him as though in a musing swoon of voluptuous ecstasy" (p. 265). In a direct sense, of course, his concept of evil is rendered more actual by the story of sexual horror he has just heard in Temple's bedroom. But his horror is not occasioned alone by Popeye's unnatural act; on an elemental level, Horace is appalled by natural sexuality because it is life-promoting. To him life is bad, for in its absence, evil would cease to exist. "Better for her if she were dead tonight, Horace thought, walking on. For me, too. He thought of her, Popeye, the woman, the child, Goodwin, all put into a single chamber, bare, lethal, immediate and profound: a single blotting instant between the indignation and the surprise. And I too; thinking how that were the only solution. Removed, cauterised out of the old and tragic flank of the world" (p. 265).

Fertility itself, then, is what Horace is spiritually at war with: the sex act as the giver of life and death. Inevitably, the unattainable desire of the male intellect is to be beyond the female cycle, which for him is inherently evil; and that is why his nihilism can be so strong. That is also why Horace, who prefers eternity to change, law to life, cessation to creation, rejects the sexual principle and the numinous feminine as utterly daemonic. Nonetheless, Benbow's view of the sex act as negative and destructive, while still the predominant outlook of the novel, is significantly qualified in the course of the narrative. In this modification lies the meaning and theme of *Sanctuary*.

Obversely, a part of the horror engendered in Benbow's consciousness is the result of his unconscious fascination with the instinctual drive of life. He is fully representative of the divided mind, the male principle of light straining toward self-sufficiency, and the feminine principle of darkness spiralling steadily downward into light's extinction. The circumambient life of the anima will permit consciousness to emerge into light, insofar as it acknowledges its source. But where the male consciousness pursues too strongly its spiritual independence, a counterbalancing tendency in the feminine unconscious seeks to subvert its rival, drawing it into self-destructive drunkenness. Negatively, the maternal unconscious reasserts its dominance in various forms: madness, incest, impotence, stupor. All lead inexorably to ego-annihilation. Benbow's impotence of intellect, his being cut off from the creative sources of life has been noted before. But there exists in his psyche's darker half an actual impulse toward destruction. Incest lurks there, at best half-hidden, although his conscious mind is struggling to repress that desire by projecting his guilt—the intellectual construct of sin—onto the object of provocation, his stepdaughter, Little Belle.

> He was thinking of the grape arbor in Kinston, of summer twilight and the murmur of voices darkening into silence as he approached, who meant them, her, no harm; who meant her less than harm, good God; darkening into the pale whisper of her white dress, of the delicate and urgent mammalian whisper of that curious small flesh which he had not begot and in which appeared to be vatted delicately some seething sympathy with the blossoming grape.
>
> He moved, suddenly. As of its own accord the photograph had shifted, slipping a little from its precarious balancing against the book. The image blurred into the highlight, like something familiar seen beneath disturbed though clear water; he looked at the familiar image with a kind of quiet horror and despair, at a face suddenly older in sin than he would ever be, a face more blurred than sweet, at eyes more secret than soft. (p. 200)

Little Belle's symbolic association with the vatted liquid of the seething grape anticipates the description of Eula Varner in *The Hamlet*: "Her entire appearance suggested some symbology out of the old Dionysic [*sic*] times—honey in sunlight and bursting grapes, the writhen bleeding of the crushed fecundated vine beneath the hard rapacious trampling goat-hoof." But where Eula Varner is become little more than an emblem of mammalian fecundity—the glandular love goddess made over into the chattel of Flem Snopes—Little Belle vitally represents for Horace the creative and destructive goddess out of the old Dionysiac times, the bearer of the mad frenzy. For the grape symbology implicitly suggests his intoxication with her dangerous beauty, his desire for uroboric incest leading to a self-destructive drunkenness. He is saved momentarily by consciousness; he displaces all the evil outside of himself, recognizing in the girl, and perhaps in all womankind, agents rather than victims of the world's sin. By the time he has heard the story of Temple's rape, however, his intellect is convulsed and rendered useless by nausea. He looks at his stepdaughter's photograph once again, and he slips back unwittingly into what has been persistently half-hid: "The face appeared to breathe in his palms in a shallow bath of highlight, beneath the slow, smoke-like tongues of invisible honeysuckle. Almost palpable enough to be seen, the scent filled the room and the small face seemed to swoon in a voluptuous languor, blurring still more, fading, leaving upon his eye a soft and fading aftermath of invitation and voluptuous promise and secret affirmation like a scent itself" (pp. 267–68). The same honeysuckle smoke in which he has seen the world perishing now licks at him with "smokelike tongues" of incestuous invitation.

Finally, crucially, Horace's continuing unconscious fantasy identifies Little Belle and Temple Drake, the two of them brought together by a photograph and the recollection of rattling shucks, and focused now into one composite image, "bound naked on her back on a flat car moving at speed through a black tunnel, the blackness streaming in rigid threads overhead, a roar of iron wheels in her ears. The car shot bodily from the tunnel in a long upward slant, the darkness overhead now shredded with parallel attenuations of living fire, toward a crescendo like a held breath, an interval in which she would swing faintly and lazily in nothingness filled with pale, myriad points of light. Far beneath her she could hear the faint, furious uproar of the shucks" (p. 268). Only now, Horace has himself become the terrified victim, a supine sacrifice to the destructive sex goddess. As he retches in the lavatory, he literally assumes a feminine identity, at once suggested by the change in pronoun genders. The act of vomiting his own bile is transformed into "she watched something black and furious go roaring out of her pale body" (p. 268).

The racing tunnel of blackness, whether it signifies uterine regression or regression into the life of the unconscious, still marks the rape of Horace's consciousness by the violent sexual force of the feminine. It seems, in other words, that the place of intellect in his psyche has been usurped by a controlling anima. For in a curious reversal, he has become passively feminine, reverting into darkness from light, taking the place now of Temple and Little Belle, himself assaulted by the dangerous potency which is borne within them. His immediate sexual horror then has a double origin: the incestuous promise leading into dissolution and death, and the forcible rape of intellect quashing his ego-identity. Either way, he is left subject to the dominant power of the archetype and its sexual principle. This horror exhibited by Horace must not be thought of as mere empathy for Temple in her ordeal; Temple's "terror," as we shall see, is qualitatively different. Horace's collapse, on the other hand, is the precursor of his acquiescence beneath the horrible visage of the black-hatted woman; it is further evidence too of her long-standing control.

After the failure of law and the male intellect in Lee Goodwin's trial, Horace reaches the nadir of his anti-vital despondency: "There was still a little snow of locust blooms on the mounting drive. 'It does last,' Horace said. 'Spring does. You'd almost think there was some purpose to it' " (p. 350). The last we see of him, he has relapsed into the pull of the incestuous promise, listening first in vague disquiet to Little Belle's breathing on the telephone, and then to the breathlessness of her sexual scuffling. Horace has been brought back fully within the encompassing life of the feminine now, but only to be devoured by it. For in Benbow, the male spiritual principle has lost its proper right to participate in the creative life of the anima; he is psychically doomed to continuing sterile desire. Irrevocably, then, consciousness has lost its struggle with the negative elementary character of the Great Goddess; the Little Belle-Temple figure awaits him finally as a spiritless and incestuous womb of death.

It is no accident that Benbow's final role should be that of a central intelligence vanquished by supra-intelligent forces. The violent destruction, however, of the four other men—Tommy and Popeye included—can hardly be said to be caused by their participation in a male spiritual principle. The only apparent relation they have to Horace is a common attitude toward sex, and therein, the female principle. Popeye's physical sterility, for example, is the perfect correlative to Benbow's sterility of consciousness, his corncob rape the counterpart to the other's anti-vital despair. Horace sums up this mutual male dilemma in purely intellectual terms; the other men express their attitudes in action, and they in turn are acted upon by the woman. From the inclusive male point of view, then, sex might appear to be the real antagonist of the story, while from the finally dominant feminine perspective, Horace and his alter egos will not even attain to protagonist status. The growth of that feminine perspective toward ascendancy must be explored before turning in conclusion to its effect upon Tommy, Red, Goodwin, and Popeye.

At first sight, Temple Drake appears to be a flapper created out of the last whimper of the Roaring Twenties. She is an overpainted, overdaring, much-sought-after prize in the college dating game, and she is always on the run during week nights—away from the campus and studious men to whom cars are not permitted—toward the town and local boys and the joyrides of the automotive age. These are the predispositions of her character. As for her story, her placement in a narrative development, she is a glittering and hovering coquette who is raped in cringing terror through grossly unnatural means and carried off into virtual prostitution, meanwhile discovering that she has all along consented to it, even enjoyed it, and that her affinity for evil is absolute, to the point of aiding, abetting, and even willing the evil end of men variously involved in her debauching. Presumably, this is the character served up with a garnish of horror to a vague mass audience. In this form, it is a story of sin without redemption, told for the sake of the sin itself.

But the readers of plot alone may have missed the symbolic qualities of *Sanctuary* which transform its meaning and purpose. From the outset, the characterization of Temple proceeds from a readily apprehended social world into a disturbing and not so easily distilled dimension of symbols: "On alternate Saturday evenings, at the Letter Club dances, or on the occasion of the three formal yearly balls, the town boys, lounging in attitudes of belligerent casualness, with their identical hats and up-turned collars, watched her enter the gymnasium upon black collegiate arms and vanish in a swirling glitter upon a glittering swirl of music, with her high delicate head and her bold painted mouth and soft chin, her eyes blankly right and left looking, cool, predatory and discreet" (p. 32). Amidst the social swirl and glitter and the conventional obeisance to proprieties, there is a chilling aura surrounding Temple, not contained alone in the carnivorous adjective "predatory," but centred certainly in the blank, cool eyes which look from side to side still seeing.

In a bedroom later on at the Old Frenchman place, as Tommy stares through the window at her, "she lifted her head and looked directly at him, her eyes calm and empty as two holes" (p. 82). The effective impression of character, so often conveyed by Faulkner through the quality of eyes, in this case suggests by vacancy or nonpresence the frightening idea that there is no human being, or perhaps something more than human, behind the taut mask of Temple's features. Immediately thereafter, the concatenation of destructive images is renewed: "She rose from the bed and removed her coat and stood motionless, arrowlike in her scant dress" (p. 82); upon reviewing her story in Miss Reba's house, her mouth will be "painted into a savage cupid's bow" (p. 256); but returning to that night spent on the Old Frenchman place, "In a single motion she was out of it, crouching a little, match-thin in her scant undergarments" (p. 82). Soon thereafter, the sound of Popeye's shooting of Tommy will revert to her: "To Temple, sitting in the cottonseed-hulls and the corncobs, the sound was no louder than the striking of a match" (p. 121). Finally, the thinness of her body itself suggests, in psychic terms, her destructive character; the fullness and massiveness of the nourishing good mother, closely identified with earth, is entirely absent from the portrait of Temple. It might appear that she is constitutionally disposed toward the person of the destroying goddess; one wonders then why the negative side of the archetype should be manifest before it is given cause. It is important to remember, at this point, that the symbol complex surrounding Temple is also the product, on every occasion, of a male perceiver; each man who looks at her appears somehow to evoke her dangerous appearance.

The more demanding question is why Temple does not once flee from danger herself, not from the Old Frenchman house, nor from the brothel, nor at last from the nightclub. By failing to exercise her power to absent herself, she leaves a trail of continuous carnage behind her. Without doubt, she is, in her own mind, terrified throughout. But she is also fascinated, poised between inviolacy and violation. The story re-counted to Horace in Miss Reba's house returns obsessively to her night of terror before the rape took place: "That was the only part of the whole experience which appeared to have left any impression on her at all: the night which she had spent in comparative inviolation" (pp. 257–58). But "suddenly Horace realised that she was recounting the experience with actual pride, a sort of naïve and impersonal vanity, as though she were making it up, looking from him to Miss Reba with quick, darting glances like a dog driving two cattle along the lane" (p. 259).

This pride of Temple's, or better, her "impersonal vanity" indicates something here that is at first glance unfathomable. It represents more than having been a violent centre of attraction that night on the Old Frenchman place; this much becomes clear during the prelude of the rape itself. Lying in the darkness with Popeye's hand fumbling inside her knickers and her skin jerking ahead of it like flying fish before a boat, she seems driven to the extremity of terror, falling desperately back on fantasy to prevent the advancing encroachment. At first, through the energy of will alone, she seeks to change the gender of her vulnerable female organs, in the confident belief that not even Popeye would have anything to do with a little boy. But when the longed-for penis fails to sprout, she conjures up a self-pitying vision of herself in a coffin, veiled in white like a bride (the matriarchate's vision of the marriage of death— ravishment by the hostile and alien male), crying because "they had put shucks in the coffin where I was dead" (p. 263). A prophetic irony, of course, transforms the cornshucks of the mattress into the corncob of the following morning. Nevertheless, Temple now repeats the silent ad-monition she had thought to say when Popeye first entered the bedroom: "But I kept on saying Coward! Coward! Touch me, coward! I got mad, because he was so long doing it. I'd talk to him. I'd say Do you think I'm going to lie here all night, just waiting on you? I'd say" (p. 263). Then, almost proleptically, Popeye is metamorphosed into a tiny "black thing," male and utterly subordinate to a great ogress of a schoolteacher with "iron gray hair," "all big up here like women get" (pp. 263–64).

Unquestionably, the outcome of the narrative suggests that Temple's fantasy at this point is close to prophetic vision. At the very least, her motivation is now ambivalent. On the one hand, it seems that her fear of genital injury is the correlative to a male sense of impotence, of complete helplessness. On the other hand, it is clear that she is also, from her deepest being, tempting Popeye to her violation and the violence that will follow it. The problem, if it is at all a problem, in Temple's characterization is that she is unconscious of herself as an incarnation of numinous forces. Insofar as she participates in the male element of consciousness, she is terrified. On the fundamental level of the unconscious, however, she draws the male world toward annihilation. Her later pride, then, is impersonal precisely because it is unconscious: her ego does not enter into it. This denial of Temple's personal motivation leads directly to her more decisive mythic motivation. Her rape—which is the focal point of her story—is a sort of catalyst precipitating this transition to impersonality; the events leading up to it reduce her part in ego-consciousness and heighten her symbolic characterization.

If one considers Temple's perspective in its developmental stages, it can be said that prior to her rape, her state of consciousness is patriarchal. Put another way, when she privately appeals for help, she tries to pray conventionally to a male deity: "But she could not think of a single designation for the heavenly father, so she began to say 'My father's a judge; my father's a judge' over and over until Goodwin ran lightly into the room" (p. 60). The comedy of an unwitting pagan goddess trying unsuccessfully to recall the heavenly father's name is steel-bladed and double-edged. For the male element of rationality is made ludicrous, caught praying to a human and social father, thus casting implicit doubt on the existence—much less the efficacy—of a "heavenly father." The abject helplessness of the patriarchal power is portrayed even more ludicrously in the moment of the rape—again through Temple's choice of a father to whom she can pray:

> She could hear silence in a thick rustling as he moved toward her through it, thrusting it aside, and she began to say Something is going to happen to me. She was saying it to the old man with the yellow clots for eyes. "Something is happening to me!" she screamed at him, sitting in his chair in the sunlight, his hands crossed on the top of the stick. "I told you it was!" she screamed, voiding the words like hot silent bubbles into the bright silence about them until he turned his head and the two phlegm-clots above her where she lay tossing and thrashing on the rough, sunny boards. "I told you! I told you all the time!" (p. 122)

In actuality, the old man sits on the porch of the house, several hundred feet from the barn where Temple lies thrashing. He nevertheless becomes transformed in her fantasy to a figure who looks, god-like, down from above her, sightless, silent, repulsive, and powerless. The "impotent" old man marks an end of a patriarchal-psychic situation in Temple; the forces of the matriarchate begin from this moment henceforth to grow into final dominance, until the male world is held totally thrall. And Temple is in fact given justifiable sway over that masculine element, beyond even her natural proclivities as a destroying goddess.

Tommy is her earliest victim. He tells Temple, ". . . Lee says hit wont hurt you none. All you got to do is lay down . . ." (p. 118, Faulkner's ellipses). "Then she felt his hand clumsily on her thigh. '. . . says hit wont hurt you none. All you got to do is . . .' " (p. 118, Faulkner's ellipses). His slow yearning for her is easily converted into protectiveness, without ever lessening the sluggish fire of his desire: "He squatted there, his hip lifted a little, until Goodwin went back into the house. Then he sighed, expelling his breath, and he looked at the blank door of the crib and again his eyes glowed with a diffident, groping, hungry fire and he began to rub his hands slowly on his shanks, rocking a little from side to side. Then he ceased, became rigid, and watched Goodwin move swiftly across the corner of the house and into the cedars" (pp. 119–20). Not even the mindless Tommy is free of a kind of conscious lust. Popeye shoots him because of his quietly possessive passion.

Red, the nightclub bouncer, furnishes stud service for Popeye on demand in a Memphis brothel, itself a kind of comic adjunct to a patriarchal world. Minnie, a maid in the house, provides us with an unforgettable tableau: "the two of them [Temple and Red] would be nekkid as two snakes, and Popeye hanging over the foot of the bed without even his hat took off, making a kind of whinnying sound" (pp. 311–12). This obscene portrait must be examined apart from Red's personal part in it. Once Red grows warm in his work, however, Popeye drills a bullet hole in his forehead. The mortal Temple, who has turned "wild as a young mare" (p. 311) under the bouncer's good offices, says quite the wrong thing to Popeye in a frenzied attempt to perserve her lover: " 'He's a better man than you are!' Temple said shrilly. 'You're not even a man! . . . Dont you wish you were Red? Dont you? Dont you wish you could do what he can do? Dont you wish he was the one watching us instead of you?' " (pp. 278–80). In spite of her physical desire for Red, the undercurrent of her passion is revealed in not-surprising terms: "He came toward her. She did not move. Her eyes began to grow darker and darker, lifting into her skull above a *half moon* of white, without focus, with the *blank rigidity* of a *statue's eyes*. She began to say Ah-ah-ah-ah in an expiring voice, her body *arching* slowly backward as though faced by an exquisite torture. When he touched her she sprang like a *bow*, hurling herself upon him, her mouth gaped and ugly like that of a *dying* fish as she *writhed* her loins against him" (p. 287, emphasis mine). The point of the italicized words is to recall their previous symbolic use in connection with Temple's character-disposition, and with Horace's vision of the destructive power of the archetypal feminine. Their renewed orchestration at this point, where even Temple supposes that she supports the man, only underscores her hidden but controlling motives.

Lee Goodwin, the third victim in chronological sequence, gets drunk on the Old Frenchman place and, stealing into the woods, looks (Actaeon-like) upon Temple's excremental nakedness. Later, he stalks barnward through the trees with rapacious intent. It is obvious what is on his mind; he has slapped Ruby down for standing in his way, and he has spelled out the nature of the act to Tommy who gives his mental assent. Goodwin is destroyed finally in terrible fury, and it seems now that there is a mythological reason for it.

Each of these interlocked instances is of one piece with Popeye's pressing a corncob into sexual service. They all are emblematic of a sort of sex which has gotten into consciousness and turned male, unnatural, infertile. The physical sterility of Popeye's unnatural implement serves supremely as an objective correlative of Benbow's sterile understanding. In different ways, they share the same disease of intellect—mind dissociated from its creative source. Correspondingly, Popeye leaning over the foot of the bed and whinnying in impotence is only one more example of head having usurped the sexual principle of life.

This mythic reason for the violent destruction of four men and the moral-intellectual collapse of another is stressed in the novel by an interesting reinterpretation of the myth of the Fall—itself related to Minnie's image of Popeye watching (Teiresias-like) the man and woman "nekkid as two snakes." Temple, in the darkness of her Memphis bedroom, is reviewing the hour for dressing for a dance back in her college dormitory:

> The worst one of all said boys thought all girls were ugly except when they were dressed. She said the Snake had been seeing Eve for several days and never noticed her until Adam made her put on a fig leaf. How do you know? they said, and she said because the Snake was there before Adam, because he was the first one thrown out of heaven; he was there all the time. But that wasn't what they meant and they said, How do you know? ... until she told them and held up her hand and swore she had. That was when the youngest one turned and ran out of the room. She locked herself in the bath and they could hear her being sick. (pp. 181–82)

The whole movement of the novel justifies this claim that Adam, not Eve, brought about the Fall. His sin was getting sex into his consciousness, covering up Eve's genitals, and consequently drawing the serpent into the act. The male intellect, then, which violates the naturalness of the conjunctive principle of life, is the first treacherous step into perdition. That, says the artist of *Sanctuary*, is the true version of the myth of the Fall.

... Interestingly enough, the reaction of the girls in Temple's dormitory— ... their participation in the male world of intellect— predicates the same violence, horror, and nausea found among the men. Through the light powder in the air the eyes of the girls, which pin back the non-virgin against the dressing table, look "like knives until you could almost watch her flesh where the eyes were touching it, and her eyes in her ugly face courageous and frightened and daring" (p. 182); the youngest of them, when she understands the truth, like Horace retches in the bathroom.

Man, however, attempts to live completely in a world of under-standing; so in the "fallen" world of knowledge, it is man who pays the real price for "sin." The novel is the proof of that: as each man in turn violates the feminine principle of life (the sanctuary) by the profane deed of thought, he is harried down and punished according to the gravity of his sacrilege. Temple, whose name seems at first subtly ironic, is revealed more and more as a true and terrible temple; from the moment of her profaning by consciousness, she begins to assume her unconsciously destructive character.

Before turning to the implications of draconian justice in the novel, two further matters concerning the male contamination of sex must be raised. Since appearances such as Temple's in *Sanctuary* are not what they seem at first, one might better appreciate what otherwise would be an awkward concluding chapter in the novel, introducing Popeye's origins only after his life is ended. Most critics have noted the metallic, machine-like imagery associated with Popeye, "that vicious depthless quality of stamped tin" (p. 2) which so effectively heightens his villainy. Yet in conclusion, new information is given about the man which tends to confirm him as Temple's agent or active element, instead of as the self-willed actor. Popeye's weakness, his ascetic aversion to alcohol, his viciousness, his actual physical impotence, are all attributed to an out-rage perpetrated upon his mother: "What with the hard work and the lack of fresh air, diversion, and the disease, the legacy which her brief husband had left her, she was not in any condition to stand shock, and there were times when she still believed that the child had perished, even though she held it in her arms crooning above it. Popeye might well have been dead" (p. 368). We are forced, almost with a sense of shock, to the recognition that Popeye's life has been all along determined. The very act of his existence is retribution for the sexual disease his father has bequeathed to him. And his role is configured from the outset in the icon of the Pietà, in his association with the mother of death.

Even the product of a physically healthy union, Ruby's child fathered by Lee, is contaminated, however, totally blighted: "The child lay on the bed, its eyes shut, flushed and sweating, its curled hands above its head in the attitude of one crucified, breathing in short whistling gasps" (p. 160). The only possible explanation is a mythic one: Goodwin, the child's father, has always regarded woman as the object of lust. Long before he purposes Temple's rape, he has killed a soldier over a black woman in the Philippines. So in a manner similar to Popeye's father (though spiritually instead of physically), he seems to have bequeathed his sexual contamination. The father thus "crucifies," without power of resurrection, his own son.

Accordingly, it must be concluded that the male imbalance of sexual consciousness in *Sanctuary* is responsible for the eruption of the negative side of the archetype. Where the feminine is violated by the prying intellect, where she is degraded into little more than an object of male gratification, there will retribution be meted out in mind-annihilating fury. The justice served upon Tommy, Red, Goodwin, Popeye, and even Benbow is draconian in the sense that it is rigorous; it is not, however, punishment for a trifling crime. However slight the offenses are of every man but Popeye, they represent a sacrilege against the basis of being; they must be punished. In the nemesis which follows, nonetheless, *Sanctuary* approaches the *götterdämmerung* of Faulkner's creation.

We come full circle to the despairing tone of the novel. The outlook propagated by this story is the bleakest, perhaps the most oppressive, in all of Faulkner's work. Even the despondency of *The Sound and the Fury*—the hopelessness which is evident as an aftermath of the blocking of Caddy's transformative character, and of her conversion into the destructive face of the archetype—is at least partially overcome in Dilsey, the finally positive representation of the Great Mother. When, however, in *Sanctuary*, the archetype offers to be similarly split, no amelioration from it is permitted by the all-powerful witch face of the goddess.

Ruby Lamar should configure the symbolic presence of the loving mother in the novel. Her name implies that she is the primordial Aphrodite, the treasure (jewel) of the sea. Time and again, she is almost portrayed as the primitive madonna: "The child whimpered, stirred. The woman stopped and changed it and took the bottle from beneath her flank and fed it. Then she leaned forward carefully and looked into Goodwin's face. 'He's asleep,' she whispered" (p. 329). She is not, however, permitted to breastfeed her son; she can only heat the bottle with her flank. The reason for this symbolic ambivalence is made quite apparent in the narrative. Once, to get her common-law husband out of Leavenworth, she unquestioningly gives herself for two months to a reprobate lawyer. Without hesitation, she expects to pay Benbow in the same currency. Benbow's response says more about himself than about her: " 'Can you stupid mammals never believe that any man, every man—You thought that was what I was coming for? You thought that if I had intended to, I'd have waited this long?' " (p. 330). Her reply is perfectly characteristic: " 'It wouldn't have done you any good if you hadn't waited.' " Horace's refusal, though noble, discloses in "you mammals" his revulsion once more, his disgust for the sexual principle and the primal nature of woman. But that primal nature seems to have atrophied in her destitute prostitution; she has been an all too willing accomplice to Goodwin's degradation of her power.

If the symbols surrounding Ruby tend toward a portrait of the good mother, the mythos projecting her activity does not. The powers of life she represents are weak. Nothing indicates that more clearly than her confrontation with Temple on the Old Frenchman place: "She returned and drew another chair up to the stove and spread the two remaining cloths and the undergarment on it, and sat again and laid the child across her lap. It wailed. 'Hush,' she said, 'hush, now' her face in the lamplight taking a serene, brooding quality" (pp. 69–70). Despite her spoken scorn for the college girl, we find in contrast the following forceful image: "A thin whisper of shadow cupped its head and lay moist upon its brow; one thin arm, upflung, lay curl-palmed beside its cheek. Temple stooped above the box. 'He's going to die,' Temple whispered. Bending, her shadow loomed high upon the wall, her coat shapeless, her hat tilted monstrously above a monstrous escaping of hair. 'Poor little baby,' she whispered, 'poor little baby' " (p. 73). On a Saturday night in May of no particular year, within a gutted farmhouse of a remote sector of north Mississippi, the artist chisels in a few brief strokes two figures in cosmic opposition. Beyond all doubt, the monstrous forces of death shadowed from the outset in Temple Drake are much more potent than the placid and serene principle of life flickering on the face of Ruby Lamar. The only explanation for this given situation seems to be the mythic one: Ruby has vitiated her own life-giving potency, both in her working out of legal fees and in her marriage to a culpable husband.

Temple's unconscious motivation, on the other hand, makes her own object-desirability a plague rather than a payment, a lure instead of a love bond. She is at once protagonist and antagonist. Her influence upon the characters who are most sympathetic (Tommy, Goodwin, Benbow) is devastating, hence antagonistic; yet her very negativity serves as a mythic redress and a moral purging. She is also the protagonist in the sense of being the leading figure of the story; by the end of the novel, she is mistress of both cosmic and social forces, including the temporal energies of Jefferson, Mississippi. Narcissa Benbow, for example, shares no symbolic part in the archetype; but she and her Baptist kind have acted as unwitting instruments of a numinous character they do not even come in contact with. They drive Ruby in the name of respectability out of Horace's house, out of the local hotel, and finally out of the town. Their cohort, Eustace Graham, the corrupt district attorney, utters conventional, even patriarchal, social platitudes in the prosecution of his case: " 'You have just heard the testimony of the chemist and the gynecologist—who is, as you gentlemen know, an authority on the most sacred affairs of that most sacred thing in life: womanhood—who says that this is no longer a matter for the hangman, but for a bonfire of gasoline—' " (p. 340). Faulkner's irony is brutally incisive, for womanhood, as we have seen, is the most sacred thing in life. The fathers and brothers responding to Graham's appeal, however, believe they act out of social verities: that the violation of a uterus upsets the law of patrilineal succession and the mores of marriageable virginity. Perhaps the archetypal feminine alone can comprehend their subservience to her darker, unconscious motive-power. In any event, they serve the cause of impotent legal justice, at the same time that they are made instruments of a terrible mythic justice, where even the thought is punished as the deed.

For reasons, then, which must ultimately defy comprehension, it seems that the destroying goddess will vanquish creation. The weakened aspect of the good mother is not able to outface the terrible feminine; Ruby Lamar is in every way overridden by Temple Drake, at last giving up her man to the furious mob. The only concrete hope left for life and continuance lies in the final portrait of her, sitting in the courtroom: "The child made a fretful sound, whimpering. 'Hush,' the woman said. 'Shhhhhhhh' " (p. 348). The more intangible hope of *Sanctuary* must lie in its prophetic warning and its apocalyptic message. The final scene of Temple in Luxembourg Gardens brings impenitent mankind to the verge—if not the midst—of *götterdämmerung*, the duration of which will be no more than "the season of rain and death." In this limited sense, *Sanctuary* is an instructive and a deeply positive work.

Sanctuary: Style As Vision

by Arthur F. Kinney

Sanctuary juxtaposes the worlds of Memphis, Tennessee, and Jefferson, Mississippi, as they are embodied by Popeye and Horace Benbow. Their confrontation is radically imaged only once, in the opening of the novel which is set at a third location, the natural spring on the Old Frenchman place, where Horace pauses to drink. . . . By all counts, this is an astonishing and bewildering scene. No two men could seem at first more unlike: the "bloodless" Popeye, looking like "stamped tin," his cigarette slanting from a chinless face, carrying a gun; the "tall, thin" Horace Benbow with his tweed coat and gray flannel trousers, carrying a book. Horace's clothes are professional, neat and comfortable; Popeye's are slick and tight, and look artificial even in the sunlight. Horace has stopped for a drink of natural water and to listen to the birds. Popeye pays no attention to the birds, may not know what kind they are, and spits into the water; his element is fire, he is a chain smoker. Although Horace attempts a formal yet polite conversation, Popeye remains sullen and laconic. While Horace is deliberate and formal, Popeye remains sneaky, mysterious, unpredictable. There would seem to be nothing to draw them together or to hold them there, yet we are told they remain, staring at each other across the reflecting water, for *two hours*. We cannot say why, for Horace is en route to Jefferson and Popeye, everywhere else an impatient man, could force Horace on with the actual threat of his revolver. Even though our perspective shifts, midway, from Horace's side of the spring to Popeye's, we are given no answers; all we know is that in some profound way these two men attract each other. From the outset, *Sanctuary* asks us in what ways Popeye and Horace are doubles and in what way their confrontation serves as an introductory emblem passage to the novel.

Horace Benbow's developing narrative consciousness is the most thoughtful, yet he is also unusually naive for a man in his forties. " 'What

"*Sanctuary*: Style As Vision" (editor's title) is extracted from *Faulkner's Narrative Poetics: Style As Vision* by Arthur F. Kinney (Amherst: University of Massachusetts Press, 1978), pp. 177–94. Copyright © 1978 by Arthur F. Kinney. A portion of this essay originally appeared in the *Journal of Modern Literature* 6, No. 2 (1977) under the title "Faulkner and Flaubert." Reprinted by permission of the publisher.

sort of men have you lived with all your life?' " Lee Goodwin will ask him. " 'In a nursery?' " Horace is not only ill adjusted to the Old Frenchman place, but we learn that he has arrived there from a troubled marriage and is on his way to the family house, where he will find himself relatively unwelcome: like Popeye, he is childless and unloved; like Popeye, he is relatively homeless. His sister Narcissa, with whom he was once so close, now sees him as a meddler who threatens her comfortable respectability. She wants nothing to do with him. . . . Narcissa's attitude toward him is dictatorial and condescending, analogous to that of his wife Belle. Horace is painfully aware of this; he is vulnerable and always on the edge of self-pity. . . .

. . . Horace tells us that in leaving Belle and her daughter, " 'I had no money with me. That was part of it too, you see; I couldn't cash a check. I couldn't get off the truck and go back to town and get some money.' " This essential self-deprecation runs so deep that he is willing to assume the same posture with Senator Clarence Snopes, although he has no respect for the senator. . . .

Horace fancies himself an intellectual . . . . Although he does display some ingenuity in questioning Ruby Lamar and in tracking down Temple Drake, his thinking is pathetically shallow. When he assures Lee Goodwin that they will win his case because Lee is innocent, because " 'You've got the law, justice, civilization,' " Lee only scoffs at him. The moment is echoed once more with Ruby just before the last day of the trial. He tells her not to worry. " 'God is foolish at times, but at least He's a gentleman. Dont you know that?' " to which Ruby replies, " 'I always though of Him as a man.' " This would seem rather dense on Horace's part, since the other gentleman he has identified, Gowan Stevens, is for him the basic cause of Goodwin's difficulty—it was Gowan who first took Temple to the Old Frenchman place and then abandoned her. Yet it is not especially surprising, for Horace's chief insight through much of the novel—"Perhaps it is upon the instant that we realise, admit, that there is a logical pattern to evil, that we die"—is hardly profound, either; rather, it resembles the reaction of an adolescent who has just discovered the presence of evil and understands for the first time that not all evil is unplanned.

Ruby's remark is interesting and revealing in another way. Horace is innocent in the ways of women. Both Ruby and her baby bother him; twice he tells her she carries the child too much, misunderstanding that love and devotion are her fundamental characteristics, as her own biography with Lee should have shown him amply enough. He is ill at ease in Miss Reba's establishment; he prejudges Temple and has diffi-culty asking her questions or listening to her story and completely misjudges what she may do when she appears at the trial; and he is so distraught by her capacity for evil that he blends her with a picture of his stepdaughter upon returning to Jefferson, judging from this composite that evil is the property of women. . . . Horace sees something more . . . than Little Belle's potentiality to be Temple Drake or that, like Temple, she is corruptible. What he sees—in this scene which shows us how he has transferred his incestuous fantasies from his sister to his step-daughter—is his essential fear and ignorance of women. Because incest can only be fantasized but never realized in the respectable society he knows, Horace has until now been relatively safe in his daydreaming romanticism. But Ruby Goodwin has shown him that for many women sexual love is natural, not bound by social restrictions, and Temple has shown him that even the young enjoy their sexuality. In their implied doubles within Horace's consciousness—in Belle and in Little Belle— they have suggested to him the fundamental nature of women as well as his own naiveté. They have confirmed his story of the shrimp in Jefferson and in Memphis as well as in Kinston. Like characters in James and Conrad, Horace does not tell his story again: Faulkner now makes silence our clue. From this point forward, Horace Benbow is as much on trial in Jefferson as Lee Goodwin, and, acknowledging this, Horace grows more secretive (with his sister and with Ruby), more defensive (in his actions), and more rigid (in his blind, dumb faith in justice): he grows toward Popeye's posture in the opening passage. In working with a mounting anxiety for Lee Goodwin's exoneration, we see Horace pri-marily attempting to exonerate his own ability as a lawyer and as a man.

So much is, by the end, within the range of Horace's narrative consciousness, although he resists most of his potential re-cognition. But *Sanctuary* also relies heavily on juxtaposition, and it is our constitutive consciousness, recalling the premise that Popeye may be a secret sharer, that allows us to understand Horace even more deeply. Both Horace and Popeye are spectators rather than participants in much of life; as im-potent men, they rely either on the power of force or on the power of social and legal codes to cloak their weakness, to show the pretense of strength. Both fear nature, especially the natural instincts of women. Both fight resignation and self-defeatism through sheer will, although both are given to moments of self-pity. Popeye's spying on Temple at Miss Reba's, like Horace's continual contact with Narcissa, discloses that both of them lack confidence in what they set out with such public assurance to do. Popeye, by violence, and Horace, with his personal interest in Ruby and in his fantasies and daydreams, try to break through their fundamental isolation. Although one is a force in the Memphis underworld and the other an established personage in Jefferson society, neither feels any stable communal role. Both men are ridden by fear, self-doubt, and self-recrimination.

Further, in keeping silent about the rum-running he sees at the Old Frenchman place, Horace becomes a petty criminal himself, an accessory after the fact, and paying off Clarence Snopes for information leading to Temple, while it parallels Narcissa's tip to Eustace Graham, displays Horace's own willing corruptibility. Popeye and Horace become two sides of the same coin of inherent human evil—those who aggressively perform evil acts and those who compromise with evil or, with the best of intentions, are unable to prevent or contain it. . . . In showing us the fundamental likeness of Horace and Popeye—their true doubling—*Sanctuary* is a study in the resources of human evil.

The major narrative blocks we are asked to juxtapose in *Sanctuary* are geographically defined. Together with the Old Frenchman place, Memphis and Jefferson form a significant triptych; they are equally weighted. The Old Frenchman place is the setting for nearly all the first third of the novel; Memphis and Jefferson are the settings for the second third, linked by Horace's trip to Miss Reba's at the close; and they also provide the environment for the final third, linked at the close by Temple's journey to Jefferson. It is no accident, either, that these three environments are carefully defined and distinguished in cosmic terms in a novel which anatomizes the nature of evil and examines the possibilities for justice.

The Old Frenchman place is the most natural and earthy of the three geographies. It is the home of two "naturals"—an idiot and a feeble old blind and deaf man—as well as the home of a common-law (or natural) marriage and a child born out of wedlock. The house itself has been taken over by the weather, and the people in it eat and drink from its crops, sleep on corn-shuck mattresses, and drink water from a natural spring on the land. . . . Although we are first introduced to this land by hearing a bird and seeing a natural spring, it is the spring in which Popeye spits and the bird's notes are regular, "as though it were worked by a clock." It is an essentially forbidding landscape and one that does terrify Temple and disorient Gowan and Horace. Our last scene there is of Tommy's murder and Temple's rape.

Next to this portrait of Earth is a portrait of Memphis imaging Hell. It is the underworld we see, a world of prostitution, violence, and crime, and its description as the Inferno is nearly classical in its dimensions. . . . The outer landscape is mirrored in Temple's room. . . . This is a society beyond conventional law; it is unnatural, mechanical, and grotesque, death-ridden. It is also, startlingly, accusatory yet empty of meaning. . . . Although our chief setting is a whorehouse, we see no active sexuality, only frustration; the environment exploits, commercializes, and degrades human passion. Within the tawdry room that Miss Reba provides there is a kind of frozen quality, a routine essentially hollow that is almost Dantean. What activity there is we find both sinful and repetitive, compulsive rather than free—in the whorehouse, the Grotto (the speakeasy), and even the streets. It is the place where Popeye reveals himself. . . . In Memphis, Popeye's hellish animality, his grotesque monstrosity, seems peculiarly fitting.

In contrast to both jungle and underworld, the Old Frenchman place and Memphis, Jefferson images society—home, business, church, courtroom. As a guardian of the best of civilized values, it is as heavenly an environment as the novel can supply. Even the convicted black murderer sees it as a place which will lead him to possible salvation . . . [singing spirituals with his fellow blacks] within the shadow of a heaven tree itself. Yet the peacefulness of this scene—its sad beauty—is ironic, for the murderer has been condemned to hell by his white society, not to heaven. The useless spiritual is reflected in the crowded streets of market day where Horace sees only the hypocrisy of fancy dress; even the country folk, he tells us, are "unmistakable by the unease of their garments as well as by their method of walking, believing that town dwellers would take them for town dwellers too, not even fooling one another." Such false respectability is ironically correlative to Narcissa's anger—" 'now to deliberately mix yourself up with a woman you said yourself was a street-walker, a murderer's woman' " . . . . Such hypocrisy leads in Jefferson to a religion of the artificial, the superficial, and the false; the town's conventions are death-dealing in themselves, its characteristic moral tidiness is only a sham. But not until his bitter remark on spring at the end of his visit is Horace able to see the depth of the quiet terror evil produces in his own native community.

Thus juxtaposed, these dramatized environments—at first discrete— supply us with a sense of unified corruptibility, of decay from within. At the Old Frenchman place, natural corn is fermented into a commercial product for the underworld of Memphis; the Memphis whorehouse trade, as in the case of Fonzo and Virgil, is drawn from Jefferson; but Jefferson also sends customers out to Goodwin's house. So the point of the triptych is in the correlation of its three panels. The Goodwin family is formally constituted on the models of family life in Jefferson, and Ruby fears that Lee will be tempted instead to the ways of Memphis; while even at Memphis Miss Reba, Miss Myrtle, and Miss Lorraine ape the social customs and unknowingly parody the social conversation of Jefferson. Since the Goodwins depend on customers from Memphis and Jefferson, their lawlessness is more disguised yet analogous to the lawlessness in the other two societies. Miss Reba's pretense of marriage is no more and no less real than Ruby's; their very names seem almost interchangeable. Red's funeral is a mockery not of its own means and ends but of the formal occasion of Jefferson which it parodies, just as Fonzo and Virgil, from Jefferson, parody Temple Drake in Memphis.

Thus the decay that is so visible at the Old Frenchman place will also have its analogies in Memphis—and in Jefferson. Horace can tell his stories of the shrimp he gets for Belle and the grape arbor where Little Belle makes love regardless of where he finds himself.

These mirroring environments are doubling on a larger and more meaningful scale. This is most apparent in the ways in which people can pass back and forth among the geographies—people like Senator Clarence Snopes, Popeye, and Temple. Even Horace, who feels initial discomfort at the Old Frenchman place and in Memphis, is able to tell his autobiography at one and, hastening away from the other, analogize Temple with his own stepdaughter and thus incorporate her into his own life. But of all the characters, Temple is the one who ties this universe of decay and evil together best: everywhere she goes, she awakens in men the same reaction, the latent desire and violence that characterize them. She herself makes little distinction; she can call on her father the judge at the Old Frenchman place, she can think of Popeye as a kind of "daddy" in Memphis (since he provides for her and is her basic authority figure and sex figure, both other self and mirror), and she can meet Judge Drake in Jefferson. She can exchange Gowan for Tommy, for Popeye, for Red. The moral equivalencies here are bitter ones: the college coquette can also become the gun moll and whore. Little wonder, then, that Horace loses in championing goodness and truth in this cohesively evil world; little wonder that Temple, confronted by the illegality of the Old Frenchman place, the corruption of Memphis, and a court trial in Jefferson, is finally unable to distinguish among them and so, without hesitation, perhaps without self-knowledge, is able to perjure herself and convict Lee Goodwin. Possibly too, fittingly, Temple's perjury confirms Narcissa's view of Lee and Ruby and so secures her hypocrisy, annealing and strengthening the behavior of Jefferson society.

All three "sanctuaries" are indistinguishable in this modern, amoral world; all three are correlated finally in the violent murder in which activity in each ends: the shooting of Tommy, the slaughter of Red, the lynching of Lee. Each death replicates the others. Thus the trial which becomes the sole focus of Horace's narrative consciousness is not merely a trial to exonerate Lee Goodwin and himself, to exonerate the system of law and justice in Jefferson generally; in *Sanctuary*, mankind itself is put on trial.

. . . Temple Drake is the core character of *Sanctuary* . . . . Her rape . . . is the chief event of the novel and the focal image to which even the trial attends; clustered about the rape, several multiple perspectives converge which we as readers must reconcile.

The violence and significance of the rape are prefigured in Ruby's persistent warnings to Temple concerning her provocative innocence, for

Ruby sees in the girl, despite their difference in social class, a fundamental secret self. When Temple continually ignores her, Ruby shares her own life story, a narrative about Frank which could be mistaken . . . for an incident in Temple's own life. . . . But Ruby's instinct to protect and love others is, in the larger structure of the novel, a bitter comment on Temple; the point is that they could never be more than *mistaken* doubles.

Ruby is identified by love, Temple by its forceful perversion in the initial rape which leads to her habitual displays of fornication for Popeye, her persistent nymphomania. We are supplied with the account of Temple's rape five times . . . . The first account is by an omniscient narrator, but he stops short of the act itself; we are told Temple sees Popeye figured in a rat staring at her, and we are provided with details concerning Tommy's death, but Temple's violation is about to occur as the passage halts: " 'Something is happening to me!' " As usual, Temple confuses sex and death. Her corncrib here becomes a coffin, the corn shucks only sterile husks. Popeye holds only a stick, analogous to Judge Drake's cane in the closing scene of the novel. This epiphany, with Temple looking at Popeye in paralysis, closes the Old Frenchman place section of the novel.

The second version of Temple's rape is given us by Ruby at the midpoint of the novel; she views the rape as a singular and needless misfortune, a privileged carelessness she condemns from her world of toil.

> "Nobody wanted her out there. Lee has told them and told them they must not bring women out there, and I told her before it got dark they were not her kind of people and to get away from there. . . .
>
> But why must it have been me, us? What had I ever done to her, to her kind?"

Ruby's perspective is paired with Horace's; he makes light of it, unawares.

> "But that girl," Horace said. "She was all right. When you were coming back to the house the next morning after the baby's bottle, you saw her and knew she was all right. . . . You know she was all right."

The fourth view is Temple's recollection, which Horace hears from her at Miss Reba's in Memphis.

> Temple told him of the night she had spent in the ruined house, from the time she entered the room and tried to wedge the door with the chair, until the woman came to the bed and led her out.

That was the only part of the whole experience which appeared to
have left any impression on her at all: the night which she had spent
in comparative inviolation.

She tells not of the rape but of her own fantasizing: that she is a boy, an
old man, a corpse. At the conclusion of her narrative, she describes the
rape in a way that reveals no particularity: the sensations have been
elevated, generalized, assimilated. The final view, that of Eustace
Graham, is not given to us directly, but it is the one which Jefferson hears
and acts on; not until then can our constitutive consciousness account for
the unusual recalcitrance in Temple or her excessive bleeding. What is
common to all five accounts is the involvement of Temple; what is at
stake is the willingness and degree of her complicity. The clues for this
are not given us directly—they rarely are in Faulkner's narrative poetics
as they rarely are in James and Conrad—but through Temple's natural
attraction for Popeye on an unconscious level and her unnatural (but
relatively easy) partnership with him.

We do not know if Temple's provocative actions at the Old Frenchman place were meant for Popeye initially or for Lee or the others;
Temple does not know herself. Her actions appear indiscriminate and
naive; she seems to bring to her new landscape the same gestures she has
been accustomed to using at Ole Miss—gestures of flight, impulsiveness,
vulnerability, invitation, confusion. When she retreats to her bed of
cornhusks (and later to a corncrib) she robes and disrobes mindlessly,
shedding any moral sense, any moral responsibility. Such innocence and
arbitrariness are provocative to several men at the Old Frenchman place
save the curious and protective Tommy; but she arouses to action only
the impotent and syphilitic Popeye, one whose body is as deformed as
her moral sense. Their affinity, once discovered, is deep and mutual.
Popeye's face with its "queer, bloodless color" and his eyes which
"looked like rubber knobs" are analogous to Temple's "bold painted
mouth and soft chin, her eyes blankly right and left looking, cool,
predatory, and discreet." Popeye is drawn to Temple as he was earlier
drawn to Horace, and she invites him at the end by taunting him. Their
departure together from the Old Frenchman place seems natural to
Ruby, who sees it, and to Temple who, in looking in the car mirror, sees
both Popeye and herself. At the filling station where they stop for fuel,
Temple leaves the car to hide from college friends who might recognize
her in Dumfries, and so invite her back to Ole Miss, but she does not
think of leaving Popeye; when he finds that she is not waiting for him in
the car, he has no trouble finding her waiting for him behind a "greasy
barrel half full of scraps of metal and rubber," an object made of
material that resembles Popeye himself. From this point on, these two
corrupt, sullen, masochistic persons are always together until Temple
tries to escape to Red, Popeye's sexual surrogate.

Their pairing underlines their relationship: both are selfish, both use others with abandon. Both act compulsively, randomly, amorally. Although they pretend to an interest in material things, they have none in fact; what they seek is limited to sensual gratification. They live only for the present. So joined are they, in fact, that one of Temple's orgasms is sufficient to satisfy both of them. For some time it does not seem to bother Temple that Popeye is not a fully active sexual partner, that he whinnies his animal pleasure at mere foreplay or in observing a surrogate, nor does it disturb him. Our constitutive consciousness therefore has no difficulty in correlating Temple as a "papier-mâché Easter [toy] filled with candy" to Popeye likened to a "wax doll" or mask pulled on a string: both seem subhuman. Nor does it surprise us when, at the end of the novel, both part by going off to their parents.

The central imaging of Temple, then, is with Popeye, and at the point of abnormal rape or sexual encounter. Such a central metaphor— Temple's rape writ large, writ endlessly—shows the sterility and meaninglessness in their selfish and corrupt existences; it seems at first ironic that the gruesome analogue to Temple's burning passion for intercourse is Lee's fiery death, itself meaningless, itself an uncontrollable passion stemming from the moral impotence of Jefferson. In the novel, this is a chief point. Lee's death, like Temple's fornication, is only the outer sign of a latent violence, only the most open admission of the corruptibility and evil in men. Popeye's essential impotence before Temple's needs is directly analogous to Horace's impotence before Lee's needs, another significant way in which Popeye and Horace are twinned. But, as Temple reveals a profound affinity with Popeye, so she suggests to Horace his own most dangerous and unrecognized self: it is in *that* that Horace sees his greatest fear as he returns on the train from Memphis and in *that* which, once realized in Jefferson in Temple's perjury, causes him to collapse altogether, to cry uselessly in Narcissa's car, and to declare a savage but useless indictment on spring. Within the larger context of a triptych of landscapes that suggests all mankind . . . , the metaphor of trial in *Sanctuary* at last pulls together Horace, Popeye, and Temple, making of this insinuated congruence a severe condemnation of man's grotesque propensity for evil.

Still this does not account for the entire novel. Although we can see why Horace and Popeye were so drawn to each other at the Old Frenchman place, why the opening scene is in fact an anticipation of the larger novel, we still do not know why Popeye has come to the Goodwin homestead. It is not his element; he feels awkward and uncomfortable, he is not welcome, and his anxiety is seen when he shoots at Tommy's dog and later shoots Tommy. Goodwin runs the place well enough, and he can drive sufficient whiskey into Memphis. Why, then, is Popeye there? It is to answer this final question that, in revising *Sanctuary* for publication, Faulkner added Popeye's biography as a penultimate episode.

Popeye comes to the Old Frenchman place because he *needs* to come. Born syphilitic, a backward child, grandson of an arsonist, mentally retarded, Popeye, for all his eventual power and wealth, has never known family love. His childhood is a case book study of the aggressive and vengeful child who seeks affection and attention: in killing the lovebirds and in cutting up the half-grown kitten he not only seeks a kind of punishment for his own misbegotten self but lashes out in a general and blind hatred against what nature comes under his control. Pain and harm become for him sources of joy and solace, like Temple's cries of pain and ecstacy at orgasm. His regressive journeys home each year are another form of self-punishment, but also frantic and empty attempts at new beginnings. At the Old Frenchman place, Popeye seeks a family, and it is the family environment that Ruby maintains. In a sense, Popeye's unnatural rape of Temple is a sick attempt to begin his own family relationship; more importantly, it is, in its open admission of impotence, Popeye's greatest act of self-punishment. It is this desire to hurt himself and thus guarantee his own worthlessness that, finally, binds him to Horace and Temple. Unfortunately for Popeye, however, he can only rape Temple at the expense of Tommy's life, and this in turn convicts Lee, robbing Popeye of the one home he has found. With the Old Frenchman place gone, and with Temple returned to her father, Popeye has no place left but his mother's—and his own greatest payment, his execution. The fate which gave him such an ugly heritage now arrests him for a crime he did not commit. Popeye is at last confronted with nothing but the terror of such truth: justice mocks itself, even outside the underworld. In attempting to regularize and organize crime in Memphis, Popeye sought to order his existence, a life disrupted first by his grandmother and now, more recently, by Temple. His concern with his appearance in his last moments—" 'Fix my hair, Jack,' he said"—is the last sign he gives us, a final gesture of futility which attempts to impart dignity to his undignified life. For he sees what our constitutive consciousness establishes, that in this world the innocent are persecuted and the guilty are set free.

Popeye's biography—as well as his execution—is comprehensible and necessary; in the larger sense of the novel, his term in jail recalls the black murderer in Jefferson who said, as if for both of them—" 'Aint no place fer you in heavum! Say, Aint no place fer you in hell! Say, Aint no place fer you in jail!' "—just as his trial echoes and parodies the trial of Lee Goodwin. We find the parallel established with pointed efficiency: in both instances, we learn, the "jury was out eight minutes."

This attempt to respond to futility with a significant gesture, which is

Popeye's last act, is essentially a mockery which has its final correlation with Temple and Judge Drake in the Luxembourg Gardens of Paris. Whether they can find sanctuary in the world of this novel—either a secret or a sacred place, a place secure or a place hallowed—they too must make their response to the world of Jefferson and Jackson, Mississippi. They do so in the height of civilization; amidst a man-trimmed park, watching children play with toy boats at a man-made basin, listening to a brass band, they sit silently, the judge holding his stick as the sign of wealth and male potency in their society, Temple yawning between glances at herself in the mirror. They have displaced the natural spring of the Old Frenchman place with a more civilized milieu and with consequent boredom. Everything has happened to them—Temple has been an accessory after the fact in two murders and has committed prostitution and perjury; Judge Drake, although he does not know of all this travesty of justice, chooses his ignorance—and nothing has happened to them. She has come to resemble Narcissa Benbow more than ever, and Judge Drake still holds the bench, a position to which Horace Benbow may still aspire. Their quiet stroll and their seat in the gardens, all quite decorous and proper, unites them with conventional Yoknapatawpha and prepares them for a return to Jefferson; meanwhile, their presence does nothing to disturb the placid and routine activity of this, or their, world. They are, finally, citizens of a corroded, corrupted mankind, as they always were: in an evil world, *that* (fittingly) is their sanctuary.

The Space Between:
A Study of Faulkner's *Sanctuary*

by George Toles

... [In] the introductory paragraphs from *Sanctuary* ... we are led into an action that is already mysteriously in progress. The external particulars of the scene are enumerated and described, the fullness of the visual/tactile representation sharply contrasting ... with the complete absence of interpretation. No effort is made to acquaint us with the motives or intentions of the two men facing each other across the desolate spring; we have no way of knowing what the encounter means or what it is building up to. We notice that here ... there are certain fixed elements to which the attention is repeatedly circling back, lending a quality of suspension to the action, a sense of time moving back on itself, like a phonograph needle caught in a worn groove. . . . [T]he scene being investigated has been ... arrested at three points: Popeye standing motionless behind the screen of bushes; Horace poised to drink beside the stream; the hidden "clockwork" bird singing three notes, pausing, and repeating them in unvarying succession. . . . [There] are ... slight confusions in the ordering of a sequence of actions—what might be termed time slippages, in which the pieces of an event are arranged in such a way that they do not form a smooth progression, but rather a series of discrete phases which overlap each other and simultaneously remain visible. This method of observing action can best be explained in terms of superimpositions. Instead of a gesture or movement disappearing into the one which follows it, the "photographic eye" snaps an impression of it, which "develops" (or holds) beneath the continuing play of images.

The mind that records phenomena in this way is always out of phase with the present moment. It is as though it were never certain what it was looking for, what it was trying to determine in its view of a given scene, so that it could not keep pace with the latter's progress. The confused observer tries to focus on many segments of an event at once precisely because he has no secure basis for understanding it. Each of the inter-acting elements in the dramatic situation are potential centers around which the others might be organized. Since he cannot decide among them, he has difficulty releasing any of the elements from his transfixed gaze.

To illustrate: in the first sentence of *Sanctuary* we are told that "Popeye watched the man drinking." The second sentence, however, instead of advancing us past the first, moves us back to an indefinite point of time preceding the moment of watching just established. Now Popeye ap-pears to be watching the man "emerge from the path and kneel to drink from the spring." At the beginning of the third paragraph, the double image is further complicated by the introduction of another small time interval located between the two already presented. This time we catch the "drinking man" at the instant he leans "his face to the broken and myriad reflection of his own drinking." His next reported movement is a rising up from the water to face the man looking at him, after which we are permitted to observe Popeye from his perspective. Two paragraphs later, we are informed that "the drinking man knelt beside the spring." He retains a posture virtually identical to that which he assumed prior to the moment represented in the first sentence. Perhaps it is only at this juncture that we can be certain that we have progressed slightly past the charged, expansive instant from which we began.

One has the blurred and faintly unsettling sense of being brought to a standstill at the point where Horace discovers he is being watched, and yet paradoxically at the same time both anticipating and recovering from that instant of shock. Faulkner prevents us from feeling squarely situated in a live present throughout the passage. Time has been broken like the "shattered reflection" Horace sees in the spring. The narrator's capacity for objectivity is qualified . . . by a confusion about what is to be done with the things being surveyed. The longer an incident is contemplated, the greater its tendency to splinter into a mass of equivocal pieces. In other words, when the narrator attempts to draw closer to what is happening in an effort to give more dimension and substance to his account of a scene, he finds himself lost on a sea of spatiotemporal variables. Only when he remains in a state of unthinking detachment from the action, scanning and randomly noting the contents of a setting, . . . only then can he produce images of reality that are neither opaque nor contorted.

It is apparent, I think, from the very beginning of the novel that the narrator is more at the mercy of the world he reveals than he is in possession of it. He approaches it with a mixture of wariness and morbid curiosity, not privileged with any insight into why things take place in the manner they do, or how they are to be deciphered and judged. . . . [I]t is perhaps . . . possible to identify the side of Faulkner's consciousness given expression in *Sanctuary* with the tormented figure of Popeye, standing at the foot of Temple's bed, watching her writhe in erotic frenzy.

The voyeuristic impulse, as Karl Abraham has argued in his celebrated essay on scopophilia, has an extremely close relation to the obsessional neurotic's need for uncertainty.[1] The type of individual who finds it necessary to be engaged continually in creating fresh uncertainties to brood upon is seeking to paralyze his capacity for gaining real knowledge: he puts in its place an essentially fraudulent *desire* for knowledge, which can always be thwarted from attaining its end. A fascination with the means by which apparently simple ideas can be turned problematic and insoluble gradually devours one's interest in concrete things and the reality of one's relations to them. For the voyeur, there is similarly a greater absorption in the artificial mechanics of desire than in desire itself. He is looking for the form of a passion more intense and complete than his own, with the perhaps unrecognized object of extending the distance which separates him from the forbidden fruit of the act itself. It is the necessity of exclusion which produces first the torture, and then an excitement growing out of the torture in the voyeur's position. Again, like the individual who cultivates his doubts and feels comfortable only when he is uncertain, the voyeur submits himself to a form of suffering where nothing is ever actualized, and from which there is no possibility of release.

The former seeks to stare at his thoughts until they become so expansive and multilayered that he will be powerless to direct or resolve them. The latter endeavors to transform his eyes into his sexual organ, creating a dysfunction in which the voyeur is once again in the child's position of not knowing what his sexuality means, and trying to penetrate the grotesque enlargements of this mystery which the adult world offers him in order to give appropriate form to his instincts. The movement toward authentic passion is blocked at every point where it is attempted, since the eye can only violate others' intimacy, never inhabit it. Both the inner vision of the brooder and the prying look of the voyeur are locked to their objects by a power of alienation that has all but destroyed the power of identification. They have disciplined themselves to regard every approach to what they want as the reinforcement of an initial rejection. Their appetite for knowledge and desire is kept alive by the certainty of endless refusal. To understand the nature of this imbalance is to grasp the difficult logic of metaphor and description in *Sanctuary*.

Returning once more to the novel's opening confrontation at the

---

[1] Karl Abraham, *Selected Papers on Psychoanalysis*, trans. Douglas Bryan and Alix Strahey (London: The Hogarth Press, 1968).

spring, we can recognize two opposed impulses at work in the presentation of the action. On the one hand, there is a positive effort to close in on the scene, to give a complete rendering of it, with an acute registration not only of spatial features—the thick, drowsy atmosphere, the quality of light in the trees and shadows in the spring—but also the feeling of time passing, of each instant held until it reaches a point of saturation. On the other hand, there is an even greater effort to hold us away from the scene, to prevent it from crystallizing to such an extent that we lose our sense of distance and come to feel we have free access to it. . . . [There are] three devices Faulkner employs to maintain this quality of opaqueness: the common literary practice of withholding information about the characters; the breaking up of time, and the insistence on its strange, uneven, subjective flow, in which we have a very unsure basis for involvement ("They squatted so, facing one another across the spring, for two hours" [p. 51]); the descriptive dismemberment of persons and settings, which is the method of dislocating perceptions in such an extreme manner that things are torn apart in the very act of being called into existence.

Popeye's outrageous incarnation, which is given to the reader in segments over the space of four pages, manages to embody both the positive (clarifying) and negative (obscuring) impulses of Faulkner's expository technique. The fact that Popeye is seen from so many different vantage points and assigned so many carefully observed attributes would seem to indicate that we are getting a progressively more refined and comprehensive image. The images do not contradict one another; in fact, they form a protective alliance, which attempts to compel our acceptance of each separate distortion by referring us to all of the others like it. Faulkner is not interested in creating momentary *trompe l'oeil* effects. The number and internal consistency of these freakish manufactured emblems give them a weight and density that put them intractably in the foreground of this harsh milieu. And yet it is clearly a dominance designed to obstruct vision and comprehension rather than promote it. The demanding struggle to make imaginative connection with the images of Popeye's physiognomy gives us a steadily increasing clarity which, paradoxically, affords no illumination. The image replaces the figure being looked at, artfully satisfying our desire to see Popeye without actually showing us anything beyond the tight black suit and cigarette which genuinely identify him.

Faulkner's metaphors, then, refuse to provide anything like an immediate cognition of reality. As we follow them through, we become involved in a form of seeing which is really an unseeing, a fatiguing dispersal of attention through an atmosphere thick with crazed associations. Faulkner speaks at one point in the novel of the effect of "a sinister and meaningless photograph poorly made" (p. 138). This is a perfect description of the nature of the conversion that metaphors (and all analogous verbal constructions) are made to perform in *Sanctuary*.

In an important sense, the contortion of language provides Faulkner with a way of not surrendering to the temptations implicit in his crudely sensational subject matter. Reduced to the level of plot, *Sanctuary* is, after all, not much more than a series of grisly and garish barroom anecdotes. Instead of choosing to modify the hysterical excesses of his story, or to endow his central characters with a psychology sufficiently large and varied to make their plight something complexly felt rather than merely gestured, Faulkner decides to keep his material in the flat and raw state in which he found it. He constructs a world which can be fully articulated as a surface and then uses his style to cover that surface, to bury it under layers of ugly, disjointed tropes. These tropes seek to take over whatever they are placed in front of and to present their own denatured reality as a stronger, if not more meaningful, alternative.

Because Faulkner has conceived the action and personalities in terms of the instantly communicable, overblown mythology of pulp fiction, he is intent on siphoning the real drama, the real content of his work back into the language. The complications created at this level may be seen as an intense recoil from the impoverished elements which the sentences are asked to embody. A middle ground is posited between the sterile incident and the eye which is forced to look at it, a ground which can be filled with stray matter in excess of the immediate, creating a wild complexity in the act of watching whose purpose is to short-circuit the latter at every turn. Unexpectedly, perhaps, Faulkner's destructive style serves to invest the raw material with a form of power that I briefly alluded to earlier: the power of refusal.

Temple and Popeye; the inhabitants of the old Frenchman's Place; Miss Reba and the incredibly congested backstairs world over which she presides—all of them owe their fitful, almost involuntary kinetic life to the ways in which they refuse to accommodate the violent wrenchings which the language gives to their form and action. Faulkner's imagery is typically so fiercely punitive and monstrous that it forces rejection. One cannot compromise with it. It insists on carrying its "transgressions" to the point where they must be acknowledged and opposed. The characters in *Sanctuary* (apart from Benbow, Miss Jenny, and Ruby Lamar, who intermittently occupy a separate category) exist most fully in their struggle to escape the rhetoric, rather than the situation, pressing in on them. They seem to assert, while enduring the savage contortions of their delineation, their right to exist on a different level. Although the debased formulas which they are enacting provide them with almost no spiritual shape and with no values or choices to be expressed, nevertheless the characters do manage to issue strangled protests against the false and deadening uses to which they are put. They have no information to give one beyond the fact that there has been a wrong accusation, that this is *not* what they are. Nowhere is this denial more unmistakably expressed than in chapter 24, when the gangster Red joins Temple in a small room behind the dance hall. . . .

There is a weight of energy piled up behind this description that threatens at every moment to burst forth, to physically demolish the figure being presented. The image of the human "bow" being drawn to the point of maximum tension gives one a startling sense of the extremity of Faulkner's desire to inflict pain. It is scarcely an exaggeration to suggest that he can hardly restrain himself from prolonging the "exquisite torture" until the bent back of his victim snaps in two. Faulkner wants to entangle verbally the promptings of passion with barbed weapons, which can lacerate the body at every new phase of arousal. Each of Temple's motions is tricked out of its ostensible significance and worked into a sadist's tapestry of twitching anguish. There is a serious conflict taking place between the power of image to inflict stylized wounds and the power of the victim to repel them. One feels the accumulating strain of impotence both in the descriptive language—which is prevented from reaching the lives it is grappling for and making its imaginary cruelties real—and in the characters themselves, who are forced to inhabit a succession of expressionist designs which neither define them nor permit them any freedom. Temple's existence in the realms of experience and metaphor is identical: frantic efforts to peck her way out of the various shells in which she is imprisoned.

Earlier, I mentioned that Faulkner's qualities as an observer in this world are like those of Popeye, standing at the foot of Temple's bed in the whorehouse. By now it should be plain how firmly the connection is established. The leering, sadistic grip of the language finds its perfect correlative in the "grip" of the inflamed eye witnessing the sexual act. In neither instance is there any opportunity for the prey to escape. The excitement generated by verbal blockages and deformations closely approximates the swell of sensations (always denied a release) which Popeye experiences as he glares helplessly at Temple and whinnies. Everywhere we are given vivid stylistic equivalents of the kind of warping that presumably takes place in the formation of Popeye's mental impressions, and they are usually offered as the standard by which all transactions in the fictive environment should be judged.

The plot of *Sanctuary* is similarly structured around the ominous rigidity of Popeye's form. Temple's imprisonment at the Frenchman's Place and Miss Reba's; Lee Goodwin's period in jail during the murder trial; Horace Benbow's collapse before the double impasse of public and private defeat—the three central movements in the plot record the process by which the power and will to move are taken away. The principal characters gradually assume more and more of the lithified character of Popeye's inhuman authority. The very atmosphere thickens around them, as they exchange their original determined activity for the numbed repose of a final tableau: Temple sitting in "the sad gloom" of the Luxembourg Gardens (a Renoir setting painted over by Munch), sullenly fingering her compact; Lee Goodwin . . . as the fire swirls up at him "silently out of a peaceful void"; Horace holding a dead telephone receiver in his hands as "the light from his wife's room" falls across the hallway in which he stands, threatening to extinguish him. Each of these futile closures in the novel mirrors Popeye's own sudden impulse to withdraw formally from life, to bridge the small gap that still separates him from the inanimate.

It is worth inquiring at this point whether the style and scheme of *Sanctuary* which I have been outlining admit the possibility of any real interior dimensions for the lives of the characters. To answer this question in the affirmative, as I hope to do, necessitates an even more interesting second question about what the nature and function of these dimensions are. The . . . extraordinary passage from chapter 19, in which Horace uneasily examines the framed portrait of his stepdaughter, Little Belle, will allow me to confront both problems directly . . . .

Horace . . . is tortured by divergent conceptions of Little Belle, neither of which . . . affords even the potential of security of consolation. When he imagines her as an innocent, demurely garbed in pale white, he is agitated by a not quite conscious feeling of incestuous yearning. When, in defensive reaction to this desire, he portrays her as a smiling Lilith, "older in sin than he would ever be," he is subject to the emasculating fear that this is what always lurks beneath the "seething sympathy" of sensual promise. Benbow's alternatives . . . can do nothing but melt into each other the longer they are contemplated. Once more we see individual points of clarity articulated in such a way as to force a merger, the aim of which is to transform what is intolerably lucid into something hopelessly uncertain. The progress of reflection in *Sanctuary* (for those characters who are shown to think) is toward the same kind of intermediate space that Faulkner's style creates for itself. The mental optic, like the actual eye, is almost never fully in touch with its apparent object.

One of the most revealing elements of Horace's encounter with the photograph is the fact that although he looks directly at the "inscrutable face" of his stepdaughter, she cannot look back at him, but rather is directing her gaze at something beyond his shoulder. This oblique positioning is emblematic of the general failure of things to find their proper alignment. . . . Horace has only an indirect, slanting view of the face in the photograph; hence his inability to probe past its conflicting possibilities to a conclusive judgment. The invisible area on which Little Belle's gaze is concentrated is the space one needs to occupy in order to read her expression accurately, but it is impossible for Horace to place himself there. It exists as an imaginary center, toward which Horace's disturbed, off-angle perspectives vaguely point, but at which they will never be able to converge.

Between the false extremes which the mind proposes there is always an excluded middle to which one cannot gain access. The dynamics of conscious life for most of the characters in *Sanctuary* appears as the repeated formulation of opposed terms which are incomplete both separately and together. Their chief purpose is to bracket the empty space dividing them, which will not hold the thing that they are vainly trying to express. Faulkner makes his characters' thoughts conform in pattern and stress to his common mode of oxymoronic narrative description. Two or more contradictory elements are grouped together as a means of suggesting that what is being depicted can only be approximated, never appropriated, by the "available language." Again, the separate details of the description are not intended to identify *themselves*, but to strain toward the undefined openings between them, where the object, in its actuality, resides.

Consider Faulkner's initial, swift sketch of Temple, as she is observed by the town boys at one of the Letter Club Dances: "with her high, delicate head and her bold painted mouth and soft chin, her eyes blankly right and left looking, cool, predatory, and discreet" (p. 29). There are numerous abrasive juxtapositions within this short excerpt which impede the smooth flowing together of effects. The red slash of the painted lips is at war with the aristocratic delicacy of the head. Temple's soft chin, in turn, seems to dilute the harsh mouth's threat of aggression. Finally, her eyes, without ceasing to register blankness, embody an unresolved tension between appetite and reserve, between an impetuous heat and a calm chill. Temple's character is formed out of the "resistances," the failed points of juncture in these verbal couplings. Like Little Belle, her equivocal form is turned, in a gesture of casual repulse, toward an invisible space, forever closed to the inquiring mind that would seek her out. Her frequently enumerated and always changing qualities do not yield up a place for her spirit to inhabit. She lives, rather, in a non-place where everything is vacantly absorbed into its opposite and then just as vacantly returned. . . .

When Temple interrupts her brusque, half-insensible performance of the rituals of grooming and coquetry to respond inwardly to what is happening to her, she is able to convert every recognition into an emphatic and nearly painless denial. "Then I'm not here . . ." she tells herself after being locked in at Miss Reba's. "This is not me. Then I'm at school. I have a date tonight" (p. 148). We would be wrong, I think, to interpret these declarations as a psychic defense thrown up in panic, for they are certainly not meant to sound the depths of an emotional injury.

Rather, they should be regarded as a clear expression of the form of self-awareness which is natural to her and beyond which she has neither the impulse nor the capacity to move. Temple . . . opposes the terms of her unpleasant situation with an inverted set of terms, imagined or from life, which gives her the desired and vaguely reassuring sense of not being inside what she is doing, but without releasing her to the extent that she feels freed for anything else.

> Horace realized that she was recounting the experience with actual pride, a sort of naive and impersonal vanity, as though she were making it up. (p. 209)

Temple has moved through her ordeal, methodically joining the two mismatched halves of her experience (past and present) together, but, like a seamstress who has neglected to fasten her thread, every fresh stitch she makes in her forward motion leaves the fabrics unconnected at the other end.

This artificial line of union (between Old Miss and the Frenchman's Place; between the relative urgencies of courtship and copulation) takes hold of nothing; like the thread, it proceeds without trace. Only the bare surface of the lived events remains to be related because that was all that there ever was for her. What Temple communicates to Horace is something he would prefer not to comprehend: how she has managed to avoid being victimized in any way which would permit feelings of outrage, or even honest sympathy, to emerge. Horace is defrauded of the emotional response which he felt was almost inherent in the situation, and which was necessary to draw the perpetrated evil back somehow into an intelligible sphere of humanity. There is no person forming itself in Temple's speech—only the hum of an appliance, or the disembodied chatter of a ventriloquist's dummy. . . .

Typically, in Faulkner's other major novels, the undefined areas which are continually opening up between known quantities signify that an impressive growth has occurred, that there has been a sudden, urgent coalescence of forms and substances which briefly suspends things in a realm of momentous potential, bounded only by the limits of the imagination's ability to hold the many as one. Faulkner by this means empowers the plain-featured reality of Yoknapatawpha County to overflow into the cosmos. In *Sanctuary* this "bursting of boundaries" does not take place. The intervals which are created in both the mental and physical realms seem designed only to exclude the things abortively piling up on either side of them. The interval has become the place where meaning disappears, rather than expands. . . .

Precarious Sanctuaries: Protection and Exposure in Faulkner's Fiction

by Philip M. Weinstein

> Something might be true while being harmful and dangerous in the highest degree. Indeed, it might be a basic characteristic of existence that those who would know it completely would perish, in which case the strength of a spirit should be measured according to how much of the "truth" one could still barely endure—or to put it more clearly, to what degree one would require it to be thinned down, shrouded, sweetened, blunted, falsified.

> NIETZSCHE, *Beyond Good and Evil*

"Breathing is a sight-draft dated yesterday," says Will Varner in *The Hamlet*, and for many of Faulkner's characters that draft is being "collected." Speechless outrage, rigid immobility, "an expression at once fatalistic and of a child's astonished disappointment" (*The Sound and the Fury*), tend to characterize their encounters with brute reality. Faulkner's people—particularly his men—are not born into the world so much as catapulted into it. They hardly cease to be amazed at the otherness of their surroundings and the impossibility of fulfilling their needs.

A chasm between self and not-self is an implicit assumption of Faulkner's narratives, and the wide variety of patterns—dreams, codes, designs, edifices—that his characters construct or draw upon represent their attempt to domesticate their space, to make sense of their lives. Before order came chaos, a world alien to human need. Since the encounter with chaos is both unbearable and inescapable, the work of Faulkner exhibits a rich array of palliative forms, of fictions that bridge that factual chasm. These fictions, in their common function of orienting and validating a self in a world-not-oneself, are sanctuaries.

A sanctuary is literally a consecrated place, one devoted to the keeping of sacred things, and it is also a place of refuge and protection, of immunity. In Faulkner the idea of sanctuary assumes a range of meanings, from escapism (Horace's vases in *Sartoris*, Hightower's reveries in *Light in August)* to transcendent affirmation (the "Grecian Urn" of changeless "heart's truth" in *Go Down, Moses*). In his later fiction Faulkner tends to cast a more benign eye on sanctuaries, on the customs, pieties, and values by which an individual endures and even prevails. Will Varner's precarious "sight-draft dated yesterday," collectible on sight, mellows into Mink Snopes's reliable pact with Old Marster, valid for life. More predictable than the cosmic joker-God who seems to preside in the early fiction, Old Marster emanates from the earth itself. He wears down his creatures but does not cheat them.

In the major fiction before *Go Down, Moses*, the protagonists are less secure in their dealings with the world outside. The power of *The Sound and the Fury* and *As I Lay Dying* lies almost wholly in Faulkner's unrelenting exposure of the exigent psyche to the forces that assail it. With the exception of *Mosquitoes*, the unbearably assaulted self is at the center of the novels prior to *Light in August*. The fictionality of fictions, the false haven they propose, is everywhere emphasized. As Mr. Compson says to Quentin, "it's nature is hurting you not Caddy" (p. 143). Nature will not stay curried, will not accept the human meaning of virginity. Exploding the fictions superimposed on it, nature rampages through Caddy, emotionally paralyzes Quentin, leaves Benjy witless—in that suggestive phrase, a natural. Nature as unbridled energy explodes manmade sanctuaries, and probably the two sequences in Faulkner's work that most memorably subject man to the torrent he neither sought nor can avoid are the flood scenes in "Old Man" and *As I Lay Dying*. Indeed, *As I Lay Dying* expresses, with grotesque concentration, the forces that conspire in Faulkner's world to make life unlivable as well as the reliance upon those sanctuaries that make it livable nevertheless. . . .

Sanctuary . . . is . . . the bleakest [novel] Faulkner ever wrote. Hostile to all versions of sanctuary, the novel "refuses to satisfy our need and desire for a place to stand, an undamaged ideal, even a hint of the hope of human efficacy."[1] Barely transcending the indifference of his avowed cynicism toward *Sanctuary*, Faulkner manages during only one of the novel's episodes to achieve full imaginative identification with his materials. That episode—the psychic disintegration of Temple Drake at Frenchman's Bend—expresses with chilling power the collapse of defective sanctuaries. To take the measure of her collapse there, one begins by noting her easy mastery of a college social scene so tailored to her various "talents" as to constitute virtually a psychic cocoon, a home away from home.

[1]Joseph W. Reed, Jr., *Faulkner's Narrative* (New Haven: Yale Univ. Press, 1973), p. 63.

Like Horace's Oxford and Gowan's University of Virginia, Temple's Ole Miss is the neatly compartmentalized stage on which she wants to be seen; it is her theater of effectiveness. Within that network of arenas, regulations, and rituals of dress and behavior Temple is at home and in control. The first glimpse of her reveals her long blond legs and bold painted mouth, and those "power centers" are displayed and exploited with cool control. Look and like, her behavior says, but do not touch. Signs of danger abound, however, and the obscene scrawl with Temple's name on the lavatory wall is portentous. Such scrawling belongs to another code, and the town boys are expressing there what they would like to do to her, the desire her behavior is calculated to stimulate without fulfilling. The lavatory scrawl also suggests grossly the body's liabilities, and one of the nightmare sequences in *Sanctuary* occurs at Frenchman's Bend where Temple is huddled in the woods, trying to relieve herself privately, when she discovers herself being watched by a stranger.[2] It is a nice girl's nightmare: not the glamorous dream of lovemaking but the nightmare of being observed excreting or later being raped with a corncob. Even more brutally than in the fate of Addie Bundren, Faulkner stresses in the ordeal of Temple the physicality of the body, the futility of locating values within it and insisting on it as an inviolable sanctuary.

Frenchman's Bend is only a few miles from Jefferson, but in *Sanctuary* Faulkner treats it as another planet. Temple encounters it, as one encounters the water in *As I Lay Dying*, traumatically. Gowan Stevens, utterly drunk, drives into a tree at 20 miles per hour, and Temple is hurtled out of the car:

> She felt herself flying through the air, carrying a numbing shock upon her shoulder and a picture of two men peering from the fringe of cane at the roadside. She scrambled to her feet, her head reverted, and saw them step into the road. . . . Still running, her bones turned to water and she fell flat on her face, still running. (p. 38)

In casual antithesis to her mastery of the Ole Miss scene, Temple intrudes violently upon the wrong stage. The car, the cool Virginian, the moving legs and arms, they are all the old props but now out of control, useless, and Temple begins to "unclot." Her body will not behave properly, and throughout these Frenchman's Bend chapters she moves like a deranged wound-up toy, starting and stopping compulsively, obedient to forces beyond her control. . . . In this encounter Temple and Gowan move and speak out of a cluster of specific social values. Those

---

[2]William Rossky takes this usually loose metaphor of nightmare more literally as he applies its characteristics—paralysis, impotence, accumulating anxiety—to the novel. See "The Pattern of Nightmare in *Sanctuary*, or, Miss Reba's Dogs" [reprinted above.—ED.]

values control both perception and behavior; the new experience is accessible only in the old terms. Temple's automatic "cringing grimace," designed to get her way pleasantly through flirtation, triggers the wrong response in Popeye: he knows whores, not coquettes. Coaxing the man into thinking he will enjoy doing her a favor, appealing to his sporting instinct, caressing his masculinity via his Packard, finally offering to pay him like a servant: these are effective routine maneuvers in her adolescent world of controlled eroticism, fast cars, good times, and easy money. At Frenchman's Bend they are useless.

Her remarks about Popeye's clothes are the acme of teenage invective, but as her frustration mounts she relapses toward greater childishness. She finally resorts to tantrum, accepting spitefully the superior force of the unswayed male, submitting to him while protesting. As the narration continues, her fright deepens and her childishness becomes infantile. Trying almost hysterically to think her way into the immunity of sanctuary, she cradles Ruby's baby and wails: "And besides, my father's a ju-judge. The gu-governor comes to our house to e-eat—What a cute little bu-ba-a-by . . . if bad man hurts Temple, us'll tell the governor's soldiers, won't us?" (p. 54).

Frantic, later, after being seen relieving herself outdoors, Temple careens into the house and tells Ruby of her outrage. She notices her hand lying on the stove, springs away, is then caught by the older woman. The privacy and protection of distance or shared custom are gone; all contact has become inimical. Temple grinds Ruby's hand against the door jamb, gets free, scrambles to the barn, flies up the ladder, falls through the loose planks, and lies gasping. Then she remembers the rat. . . .

Temple has become a cornered animal. Everything in her world is jailer or violator. Ruby smothers her, the floor opens up, the rat beams passionate aggression, the corncob on which she treads will soon rape her, the door will not open. It is a world of pure abrasiveness; indeed Temple is being raped continuously, not just once by Popeye with a corncob. The disintegration of Temple Drake is the emotional center of the novel and the locus of its considerable power. In it Faulkner renders the damage that a psyche can undergo, damage analogous to the war wounds incurred "off stage" by Donald Mahon and Bayard Sartoris. The intermittent anguish of Temple metamorphoses, in *The Sound and the Fury*, into the unforgettable ordeal of Benjy and Quentin; and Temple deserves from Faulkner's critics a measure of the sympathy those two characters receive.

Usually dismissed as a nymphomaniac or a bitch who gets what she deserves, Temple actually suffers, during these extraordinary early chapters, as a full-fledged Faulkner heroine. The narrative point of view is unironic, fully committed to the protagonist's agony. In the collapse of her defective rituals of thinking and feeling, Temple is undergoing a Faulknerian initiation. She is being moved out of a sanctioned world of "licensed tranquility" into a chaotic one of meaningless terror and aggression. That she succumbs to its pressures is no indictment: few of Faulkner's early protagonists who are equally exposed fare better. The Temple Drake of the later chapters is not so much immoral as psychically damaged, tampered with. Breathing is a sight-drafted dated yesterday, and hers, figuratively speaking, was collected at Frenchman's Bend. . . .

Chronology of Important Dates
by David Minter

1825	6 July: William Clark Falkner, later "The Old Colonel," is born in Knox County, Tennessee.
1842	He arrives in Mississippi.
1843–1845	He settles in Ripley, Mississippi.
1846–1847	He serves in the Mexican War.
1847	9 July: he marries Holland Pearce.
1848	2 Sept.: John Wesley Thompson Falkner, later "The Young Colonel," is born.
1849	W. C. Falkner kills Robert Hindman, is tried and acquitted. 31 May: Holland Pearce Falkner dies.
1851	W. C. Falkner kills Erasmus W. Morris, is tried and acquitted. He publishes *The Siege of Monterrey* (an autobiographical poem) and *The Spanish Heroine* (a novel). 12 Oct.: he marries Elizabeth Houston Vance.
1861	9 Jan.: Mississippi secedes. W. C. Falkner and the Magnolia Rifles enter the Civil War.
1862	Replaced as regiment commander by John M. Stone, W. C. Falkner returns to Ripley.
1863	He forms the Partisan Rangers and reenters the war.
1869	2 Sept.: John Wesley Thompson Falkner marries Sallie McAlpine Murry, and they settle in Ripley.
1870	17 Aug.: Murry Cuthbert Falkner is born.

"Chronology of Important Dates" (editor's title) by David Minter, reprinted from *William Faulkner: His Life and Work* (Baltimore and London: Johns Hopkins University Press, 1980), pp. 255–59. Copyright © 1980 by the Johns Hopkins University Press. Reprinted by permission of the publisher.

1871	27 Nov.: Maud Butler, daughter of Leila Dean Swift and Charles Butler, is born.
1871–1872	W. C. Falkner, Richard Thurmond, and others organize a company to build a railroad.
1881–1884	W. C. Falkner writes *The White Rose of Memphis*, tours Europe, and writes *Rapid Ramblings in Europe.*
1885	J. W. T. Falkner moves his family to Oxford, Mississippi.
1889	5 Nov.: after being elected to the state legislature, W. C. Falkner is shot by Richard Thurmond. 6 Nov.: he dies.
ca. 1890	Charles Butler deserts Leila Butler, who is forced to forfeit a scholarship for studying sculpture in Rome. Murry Faulkner quits the University of Mississippi to work on the family railroad.
1896	19 Feb.: Lida Estelle Oldham is born in Bonham, Texas. 9 Nov.: Murry Falkner marries Maud Butler, and they settle in New Albany, Mississippi.
1897	25 Sept.: William Cuthbert Falkner is born.
1898	Murry Falkner is appointed treasurer of the railroad, and the family moves to Ripley.
1899	26 June: Murry C. Falkner, Jr., is born.
1901	24 Sept.: John Wesley Thompson Falkner, III, is born.
1902	J. W. T. Falkner sells the railroad. Murry Falkner moves his family to Oxford and begins shifting from job to job.
1903	Lemuel E. Oldham, his wife, Lida, and their daughters, Lida Estelle and Victoria, move from Kosciusko, Mississippi, to Oxford.
1905	William Falkner enters the first grade.
1907	1 June: Leila Swift Butler (Damuddy) dies. 15 Aug.: Dean Swift Falkner is born.
1909	William Falkner's decline in attendance and performance at school begins.
1914	He quits school after several years of increasing resistance. His long friendship with Phil Stone begins.
1915	He again begins the eleventh grade and again quits.

1916   He works briefly in his grandfather's bank but gravitates toward student activities at the University of Mississippi.

1917   His first published work, a drawing, appears in the yearbook *Ole Miss*.

1918   Estelle Oldham's parents announce her engagement to Cornell Franklin. William Falkner tries to enlist, is rejected, and leaves for New Haven, Connecticut, where he lives with Phil Stone and works for the Winchester Repeating Arms Company. June: he changes the spelling of his name from *Falkner* to *Faulkner* and enlists in the R.A.F. (Canada). 11 Nov.: World War One ends while he is still in training. Dec.: he returns to Oxford.

1919   8 Feb.: Victoria Franklin is born. Estelle Franklin visits her parents in Oxford. Faulkner works on the poems that become *The Marble Faun*. 6 Aug.: his first published poem, "L'Apres-Midi d'un Faune," appears in the *New Republic*. He enrolls at the university, where he publishes poems and drawings in student publications.

1920   He resigns from the university but continues to work with a student drama group, for which he writes *The Marionettes*.

1921   Spring: Estelle Franklin visits her parents, and Faulkner writes "Vision in Spring." Fall: he moves to New York and works in a bookstore. Dec.: he returns to Oxford as postmaster of the university post office.

1922   He serves as scoutmaster and postmaster, writes for university publications. June: he publishes "Portrait" (a poem) in the *Double Dealer*.

1923   3 Dec.: Malcolm A. Franklin is born.

1924   Faulkner is removed as scoutmaster and resigns as postmaster. 15 Dec.: Four Seas publishes *The Marble Faun*.

1925   Faulkner moves to New Orleans, writes for the *Double Dealer* and New Orleans *Times-Picayune*, becomes friends with several artists and writers, writes *Soldiers' Pay*, and falls in love with Helen Baird. 7 July: he sails for Europe where he travels in Italy, Switzerland, France, and England, lives in Paris, and writes "Elmer." Dec.: he returns to Oxford.

1926   25 Feb.: *Soldiers' Pay* is published. Splitting time between Oxford, New Orleans, and Pascagoula, Faulkner courts

Helen Baird, writes *Mosquitoes*, and collaborates on *Sherwood Anderson & Other Famous Creoles*.

1927   30 Apr.: *Mosquitoes* is published. Faulkner works on "Father Abraham" and *Flags in the Dust*, then concentrates on *Flags in the Dust*. Nov.: Horace Liveright rejects *Flags in the Dust*.

1928   Faulkner writes *The Sound and the Fury* in Oxford and revises it in New York.

1929   31 Jan.: *Sartoris*, a cut version of *Flags in the Dust*, is published. 29 Apr.: Estelle Franklin's divorce is granted. May: Faulkner finishes *Sanctuary*. 20 June: he and Estelle are married. 7 Oct.: *The Sound and the Fury* is published. 29 Oct.: Faulkner begins *As I Lay Dying*.

1930   12 Jan.: he completes revised typescript of *As I Lay Dying*. Prominent magazines begin buying his stories. He and Estelle buy an antebellum house and name it "Rowan Oak." 6 Oct.: *As I Lay Dying* is published. Faulkner revises *Sanctuary*.

1931   Jan.: Alabama Faulkner is born and dies. 9 Feb.: *Sanctuary* is published. Faulkner begins *Light in August*. 21 Sept.: *These 13* is published. Oct.: Faulkner attends a writers' conference in Charlottesville, Virginia, then spends seven weeks in New York.

1932   Feb.: he finishes *Light in August*. May: he begins his first job in Hollywood. 7 Aug.: Murry Falkner dies. Oct.: Faulkner returns to Hollywood; *Light in August* is published.

1933   Feb.: Faulkner begins flying lessons. 20 Apr.: *A Green Bough* is published. 24 June: Jill Faulkner is born. Faulkner buys an airplane.

1934   He begins the work that becomes *Absalom, Absalom!*, then writes several stories that become *The Unvanquished*. 16 Apr.: *Doctor Martino and Other Stories* is published. July: Faulkner goes to Hollywood for several weeks. Back in Oxford, he writes *Pylon*.

1935   He works on *Absalom, Absalom!* 25 Mar.: *Pylon* is published. 10 Nov.: Dean Faulkner dies. Dec.: Faulkner leaves for several weeks in Hollywood.

1936   Finishes *Absalom, Absalom!* Feb–May: he works in Hollywood. His affair with Meta Doherty, begun in 1935, deepens. June: he returns to Oxford. Late July: he returns to

Hollywood with Estelle and Jill, expecting to stay a year. 26 Oct.: *Absalom, Absalom!* is published.

1937   Late Mar. or early Apr.: Meta Doherty marries Wolfgang Rebner. May: Estelle and Jill return to Oxford. Late Aug.: Faulkner follows. Oct.: he goes to New York, where he sees Meta Rebner.

1938   15 Feb.: *The Unvanquished* is published. Faulkner buys "Greenfield Farm," writes *The Wild Palms*, and begins the Snopes trilogy.

1939   19 Jan.: *The Wild Palms* is published. Faulkner is elected to the National Institute of Arts and Letters.

1940   27 Jan.: Mammy Caroline Barr dies. 1 Apr.: *The Hamlet* is published. Faulkner writes stories that become *Go Down, Moses*.

1941   He works on *Go Down, Moses*.

1942   11 May: *Go Down, Moses* is published. Late July: Faulkner begins five-month stint in Hollywood and resumes affair with Meta Doherty.

1943   16 Jan.: he returns to Hollywood for seven months. Oct.: he begins work that becomes *A Fable*.

1944   Feb.: he returns to Hollywood for extended stay. May: he begins correspondence with Malcolm Cowley. Summer: Estelle and Jill join him for two months. Dec.: he returns to Oxford.

1945   He resumes work on his fable. June–Sept.: he works in Hollywood.

1946   Mar.: Robert Haas and Harold Ober secure his release from Warner Brothers. 29 Apr.: *The Portable Faulkner* is published.

1947   Oct.: Faulkner submits a portion of his fable, "Notes on a Horsethief," to the *Partisan Review*, which rejects it.

1948   He puts his fable aside and writes *Intruder in the Dust*. 27 Sept.: *Intruder in the Dust* is published. 23 Nov.: Faulkner is elected to the American Academy of Arts and Letters.

1949   Aug.: he meets Joan Williams. 27 Nov.: *Night's Gambit* is published.

1950   Jan.: he begins collaborations with Joan Williams on *Requiem for a Nun.* 2 Aug.: *Collected Stories* is published. 10 Nov.: Faulkner learns that he has won the Nobel Prize. Dec.: he and Jill go to Stockholm.

1951   Feb.: *Notes on a Horsethief* is published, and Faulkner goes to Hollywood for five weeks. Mid-Apr.: he leaves for Europe. 27 Sept.: *Requiem for a Nun* is published.

1952   Faulkner moves between Oxford and New York. May: he goes to Europe. Summer: he and Joan Williams become lovers. Nov.: he undergoes a series of electroshock treatments.

1953   He continues to move between Oxford and New York. Nov.: he finishes *A Fable*, dedicates it to Jill, and leaves for Europe.

1954   He remains in Europe for several months, working with Howard Hawks. In St. Moritz, he meets Jean Stein. Mar.: he learns that Joan Williams has married Ezra Bowen and that Jill wants to marry Paul Summers. Apr.: he returns to Oxford. 2 Aug.: *A Fable* is published. 6–16 Aug.: he makes his first trip for the State Department. 21 Aug.: Jill marries Paul Summers. Sept.: Faulkner goes to New York to see Jean Stein.

1955   His involvement in integration controversies intensifies. 29 July: he begins a trip for the State Department that takes him from Japan through Europe to Iceland. 14 Oct.: *Big Woods* is published. Dec.: he takes Jean Stein to Pascagoula and New Orleans.

1956   Faulkner splits time between New York and Oxford, works on *The Town*, and writes articles on integration.

1957   He becomes writer-in-residence at the University of Virginia, Charlottesville, and visits Greece for the State Department. 1 May: *The Town* is published.

1958   Jan.: Faulkner returns to the University of Virginia as writer-in-residence. Splitting time between Oxford and Charlottesville, he works on *The Mansion*.

1959   He and Estelle buy a house in Charlottesville. He attends UNESCO conference in Denver. 13 Nov.: *The Mansion* is published.

1960   16 Oct.: Maud Butler Falkner dies. Dec.: Faulkner wills his manuscripts to the William Faulkner Foundation.

1961   Apr.: he goes to Venezuela for the State Department. Summer: he makes rapid progress on *The Reivers*.

1962   4 June: *The Reivers* is published. 5 July: Faulkner enters Wright's Sanitarium in Byhalia, Mississippi. 6 July: he dies.

Notes on the Editor and Contributors

T. H. ADAMOWSKI is Professor of English at Erindale College, University of Toronto, and the author of articles on Faulkner, Lawrence, Sartre, and others in such journals as *Novel, Critical Inquiry, Mosaic, The D. H. Lawrence Review,* and *University of Toronto Quarterly.*

J. DOUGLAS CANFIELD, editor of this volume, is Professor of English at the University of Arizona and the author of a book on Nicholas Rowe and articles on Restoration and eighteenth-century literature. He has recently edited a special issue of *Arizona Quarterly* (Winter 1980), featuring work by members of the Arizona Study Group on Critical Theory and containing his article on *Go Down, Moses.*

DAVID L. FRAZIER is Professor of English at Miami University of Ohio, author of articles on American literature, especially W. D. Howells, and editor of *The Old Northwest: A Journal of Regional Life and Letters.*

ARTHUR F. KINNEY is Professor of English at the University of Massachusetts, editor of *English Literary Renaissance,* coeditor of Twayne's English Authors Series, and, besides his book on Faulkner, the author of several articles and books on Renaissance English literature.

The late LAWRENCE S. KUBIE, M.D., was a world-famous psychoanalyst and an eminent teacher at such places as the New York Psychoanalytic Institute and Columbia, Yale, and Johns Hopkins universities. During his long career, he published prolifically in the field of psychoanalysis and related sciences. Many of his papers were collected posthumously and published as *Symbol and Neurosis: Selected Papers of Lawrence S. Kubie* (1978).

THOMAS L. MCHANEY is Professor of English at Georgia State University and the author of several short stories and, recently, plays, as well as essays on nineteenth- and twentieth-century American literature and two books on Faulkner: *William Faulkner's "The Wild Palms": A Study* (1976) and *William Faulkner: A Reference Guide* (1976).

DAVID MINTER is Professor of English and Dean of Emory College, Emory University, editor of the Twentieth Century Interpretations of

Faulkner's *Light in August*, and, besides his book on Faulkner, the author of articles on American Literature and a book on style, *The Interpreted Design as a Structured Principle in American Prose* (1969).

WILLIAM ROSSKY is Professor of English and former Chairman of the Department at Temple University. He is the author of articles on the literature of the English Renaissance, especially Shakespeare, and on American literature, especially Faulkner. His articles on *The Reivers* and *As I Lay Dying* have also been reprinted in similar collections.

GEORGE TOLES is Associate Professor of English at University College, University of Manitoba, author of articles on Frank Capra in the *Canadian Review of American Studies* and on Charles Brockden Brown in *Early American Literature*, and editor of a forthcoming special issue of *Mosaic* on film and literature.

The late OLGA W. VICKERY taught at the University of Southern California. Besides authoring her seminal book on Faulkner, she coedited *Three Decades of Faulkner Criticism* (1961; with F. J. Hoffman) and *"Light in August" and the Critical Spectrum* (1971; with J. B. Vickery).

PHILIP M. WEINSTEIN is Professor of English Literature and Chairman of the Department at Swarthmore College and the author of articles on the modern novel and a book on James, *Henry James and the Requirements of the Imagination* (1971).

AUBREY WILLIAMS is Graduate Research Professor of English at the University of Florida and the author or editor of numerous articles and books on the eighteenth century, especially Pope, and on Restoration drama, especially Congreve.

DAVID WILLIAMS is Associate Professor of English at St. Paul's College, University of Manitoba, and, besides his book on Faulkner, is the author of two novels, as well as critical articles in the *Canadian Review of American Studies* and *Dalhousie Review*.

Selected Bibliography

(Works Cited in the Introduction)

Bassett, John. *William Faulkner: An Annotated Checklist of Criticism.* New York: David Lewis, 1972.

———. *William Faulkner: The Critical Heritage.* Boston: Routledge and Kegan Paul, 1975.

de Beauvoir, Simone. *La force d'age.* Paris: Gallimard, 1960.

Beck, Warren. *Faulkner Essays.* Madison: University of Wisconsin Press, 1976.

Blotner, Joseph. *Faulkner: A Biography.* 2 vols. New York: Random House, 1974.

Brooks, Cleanth. "Faulkner's *Sanctuary*: The Discovery of Evil." *Sewanee Review* (1963). Reprinted in *William Faulkner: The Yoknapatawpha Country.* New Haven: Yale University Press, 1963, pp. 116–40, 387–98.

Brown, Calvin S. "*Sanctuary*: From Confrontation to Peaceful Void." *Mosaic*, 7, No. 1 (1973), 75–95.

Camus, Albert. Letter to the editor, *Harvard Advocate*, 135 (November 1951), 21.

Creighton, Joanne V. "Self-Destructive Evil in *Sanctuary*." *Twentieth Century Literature*, 18 (1972), 259–70.

Cypher, James R. "The Tangled Sexuality of Temple Drake." *American Imago*, 19 (1962), 243–52.

Degenfelder, E. Pauline. "The Four Faces of Temple Drake: Faulkner's *Sanctuary, Requiem for a Nun*, and the Two Film Adaptations." *American Quarterly*, 28 (1976), 544–60.

Esslinger, Pat M. "No Spinach in *Sanctuary*." *Modern Fiction Studies*, 18 (1972–73), 555–58.

Faulkner, William. *Essays, Speeches, and Public Letters*, ed. James B. Meriwether. New York: Random House, 1965.

———. *The Hamlet.* 2nd ed. New York: Random House, 1964.

———. *Requiem for a Nun.* 2nd ed. New York: Vintage, 1975.

———. "Sanctuary." Holograph manuscript in William Faulkner Collections (#6074), Manuscripts Department, University of Virginia Library.

———. "Sanctuary." Carbon of typescript in William Faulkner Collections (#6074), Manuscripts Department, University of Virginia Library.

———. "Sanctuary." Page proofs in William Faulkner Collections (#6271-ag), Manuscripts Department, University of Virginia Library.

———. *Sanctuary.* New York: Jonathan Cape and Harrison Smith, 1931.

———. *Sanctuary.* Reissue of 1st ed. New York: Modern Library, 1932.

———. *Sanctuary.* 2nd ed. New York: Random House, 1962.

———. *Sanctuary.* Reissue of 2nd ed. New York: Vintage, 1967.

———. *"Sanctuary": The Original Text*, edited, with Afterword and Notes, by Noel Polk. New York: Random House, 1981.

Freud, Sigmund, *On Creativity and the Unconscious: Papers on the Psychology of Art, Literature, Love, Religion*, ed. Benjamin Nelson. New York: Harper & Row, 1958.

Guérard, Albert J. "The Misogynous Vision As High Art: Faulkner's *Sanctuary.*" *Southern Review*, 12 (1976), 215–31.

Gwynn, Frederick L., and Joseph L. Blotner, eds. *Faulkner in the University: Class Conferences at the University of Virginia, 1957–58.* Charlottesville: University Press of Virginia, 1959.

Langford, Gerald. *Faulkner's Revision of Sanctuary: A Collation of the Unrevised Galleys and the Published Book.* Austin: University of Texas Press, 1972.

Lewis, Wyndham. "The Moralist with a Corn-cob: A Study of William Faulkner." *Life and Letters*, 10 (1934), 312–28.

Malraux, André. Preface to *Sanctuaire* (1933), trans. in *Yale French Studies* (1952). Reprinted in Warren, pp. 272–74.

Mason, Robert L. "A Defense of Faulkner's *Sanctuary.*" *The Georgia Review*, 21 (1967), 430–38.

Massey, Linton. "Notes on the Unrevised Galleys of Faulkner's *Sanctuary.*" *Studies in Bibliography*, 8 (1956), 195–208.

Materassi, Mario. *I Romanzi di Faulkner.* Biblioteca di Studi Americani, 17. Rome: Edizioni Abete, 1968.

Meriwether, James B. "The Books of William Faulkner: A Guide for Students and Scholars." *Mississippi Quarterly*, 30 (1977), 417–28.

——. Some Notes on the Text of Faulkner's *Sanctuary.*" *Papers of the Bibliographical Society of America*, 55 (1961), 192–206.

Meriwether, James B., and Michael Millgate, eds. *Lion in the Garden: Interviews with William Faulkner, 1926–1962.* 1968. Reprinted Lincoln: University of Nebraska Press, 1980.

Miller, James E., Jr. "*Sanctuary*: Yoknapatawpha's Waste Land." In *The Twenties: Fiction, Poetry, Drama*, ed. Warren French. Deland, Fla.: Everett/Edwards, 1975, pp. 249–67.

Millgate, Michael. " 'A Fair Job': A Study of Faulkner's *Sanctuary.*" *Review of English Literature* (1963). Reprinted in *The Achievement of William Faulkner.* New York: Random House, 1966, pp. 113–23.

Nietzsche, Friedrich. *"The Birth of Tragedy" and "The Genealogy of Morals,"* trans. Francis Goffing. New York: Doubleday, 1956.

Nishiyama, Tamotsu. "What Really Happens in *Sanctuary.*" *Studies in English Literature* (Tokyo), 42 (1966), 235–43.

O'Donnell, George Marion. "Faulkner's Mythology." *Kenyon Review* (1939). Reprinted in Warren, pp. 23–33.

Page, Sally R. *Faulkner's Women: Characterization and Meaning.* Deland, Fla.: Everett/Edwards, 1972.

Reed, Joseph W., Jr. *Faulkner's Narrative.* New Haven: Yale University Press, 1973.

Straumann, Heinrich. *William Faulkner.* Frankfurt am Main: Athenäum Verlag, 1968.

Thompson, Lawrance. *William Faulkner: An Introduction and Interpretation.* 2nd ed. New York: Holt, 1967.

Volpe, Edmond L. *A Reader's Guide to William Faulkner.* New York: Farrar, Straus and Giroux, 1964.

Waggoner, Hyatt H. *William Faulkner: From Jefferson to the World.* Lexington: University of Kentucky Press, 1959.

Warren, Robert Penn, ed. *Faulkner: A Collection of Critical Essays.* Twentieth Century Views. Englewood Cliffs, N.J.: Prentice-Hall, 1966.